D1256705

# Understanding Love:™

*Marriage,
Still a Great Idea*

# Understanding Love:™

Marriage,
Still a Great Idea

## DR. MYLES MUNROE

**Destiny Image® Publishers, Inc.**
**P.O. Box 310**
**Shippensburg, PA 17257-0310**

"Speaking to the Purposes of God for This Generation
and for the Generations to Come"

ISBN 0-7684-2154-3

**Bahamas Faith Ministry**
**P.O. Box N9583**
**Nassau, Bahamas**

For Worldwide Distribution
Printed in the U.S.A.

This book and all other Destiny Image, Revival Press,
MercyPlace, Fresh Bread, Destiny Image Fiction,
and Treasure House books are available
at Christian bookstores and distributors worldwide.

Third Printing: 2002          Fourth Printing: 2002

For a U.S. bookstore nearest you, call **1-800-722-6774**.
For more information on foreign distributors, call **717-532-3040**.
Or reach us on the Internet:
**www.destinyimage.com**

# Dedication

$T$o my beautiful, fantastic, awesome, wonderful, sensitive wife, Ruth; your support, respect, commitment, dedication, patience, and prayers for me make me look like a good husband and father. Thank you for making the principles in this book a practical reality. Thank you for making our marriage all I expected this adventure in human relations to be. I love you.

To my precious daughter, Charisa, and my beloved son, Chairo. May your marriages be built on the principles and precepts inherent in the distilled wisdom of the time tested truths of the Word of God. May this book become my greatest wedding gift to you and your children as you embrace its precepts.

To my father and late mother, Matthias and Louise Munroe. Your marriage of over 50 years became the living model and standard for me as I observed the beauty and benefit of a marriage built on the foundation of the word of God. Thank you for teaching me how to love my wife and children.

To all the unmarried singles who desire to have the successful marriage the Creator originally intended. May the wisdom of this book contribute to this desire.

To all married couples whose desire it is to improve and enhance their relationship. May you apply the principles of this book to assist in fulfilling your vows and to experience the marriage the Creator originally intended for mankind.

To the source of all wisdom, knowledge and understanding, the Creator of the institute of marriage, my Lord and Redeemer, Jehovah Shalom, Yeshua.

# Contents

# Preface

The greatest source of human joy and pain is found in the drama of love and relationships. Marriage has always been the most common context for this drama. Today, many question the viability and validity of marriage and openly wonder if it should continue to be esteemed as the bedrock of modern social development.

The epidemic and explosive rise of the divorce rate adds further fuel to the fear, hopelessness, disillusionment, and despair people feel with regard to marriage. Many are skeptical and question their chances at success in marriage. The situation is so serious that some have opted for co-habitation without any formal contract or legal agreement, with the understanding that no commitment is involved—no strings attached. In essence, we are producing a generation whose appreciation and respect for the institution of marriage is disintegrating.

Many victims of these failed marriages and divorced families develop resentment and suppressed anger, which manifest themselves in a generational transfer of broken relationships and emotional dysfunction. Because of the fear of failure, some have plainly stated that they neither believe in marriage nor intend ever to marry. The negative press given to high profile individuals in sports, entertainment, politics and, sadly, the church, whose marriages have also fallen victim to the demise of relationships, has not helped. It has served only to further erode the respect, confidence and the high position the marriage institution once held in the social structure of our communities.

Where is this all headed? Where do we go from here? Will the institution of marriage survive the onslaught of negative reports, horror stories, and the proponents of radical society change who promote the idea that marriage has outlived its usefulness and value to human society?

I am curious: If we do away with the traditional institution of marriage, what will we replace it with? What more effective and efficient arrangement could we find to secure the level of commitment, loyalty, support, sense of community, and love necessary to meet the basic needs of the human spirit, needs such as love, a sense of belonging and importance, security and mutual respect? Over the past six thousand years no civilization or culture has produced a better concept for orderly social development than that of the traditional institution of marriage. Every society and culture has recognized an instinctive desire and need for a formal arrangement for the healthy development of families.

It is my belief that no matter how advanced man may become in science, technology, systems, and knowledge, he can never improve on the foundational precepts of marriage as the bedrock of social development. It is my conviction *that marriage is such a good idea, only God could have thought of it.*

In spite of the many failed marriages, broken homes, divorce cases and disillusioned products of failed relationships, marriage is still a good idea. In fact, it is the best idea.

## CHAPTER ONE

# *Marriage Is Like a Precious Gem*

$\mathcal{A}$ lot of people are confused about marriage these days. In the eyes of many, the institution of marriage has become irrelevant, an archaic relic of a simpler and more naïve time. They question whether marriage is still a good idea, particularly in today's more "liberated" and "enlightened" culture. Concepts such as honor, trust, faithfulness, and commitment seem old-fashioned and out of touch with modern society. Many people change partners as easily as they change shoes (and almost as frequently!).

This confusion over marriage should not surprise us, considering the bewildering barrage of worldly attitudes and philosophies that hits us at every turn. Every day books, magazines, movies, and television soap operas, sitcoms, and prime-time dramas bombard us with images of wives cheating on their husbands and husbands cheating on their wives. Unmarried men and women hop into bed with each other at the drop of a hat, and just as quickly hop out again to find their next partner.

People today shop for relationships the way they shop for clothes. They "try something on for size," and if it does not fit they simply try something else. When they find something that suits them they wear it for awhile until it fades or goes out of style. Then they throw it out or hang it up in the back of their closet and rush out to replace it.

We live in a disposable, "cast-off-and-throw-away" society that has largely lost any real sense of permanence. Ours is a world of expiration dates, limited shelf life, and planned obsolescence. Nothing is absolute. Truth exists only in the eye of the beholder and morality is the whim of the moment. In such an environment, is it any wonder that people ask, "Doesn't *anything* last anymore? Isn't there *something* I can depend on?"

One major symptom of a sick society is when we attach to our human relationships the same attitude of impersonal transience that we display toward the inanimate and disposable items that we use in everyday life. Marriage is the deepest and most intimate of all human relationships, yet even it is under assault. Is marriage still viable in modern society? Does it still make sense in our transitory world? Is marriage still a good idea?

## Marriage Is God's Idea

The answer is *yes*. Marriage *is* still a good idea because it is *God's* idea. He created it. He designed it. He established it and defined its parameters. Contrary to much contemporary thought and teaching, marriage is not a human concept. Mankind did not simply dream up marriage somewhere along the line as a convenient way of handling relationships and responsibilities between men and women or dealing with childbearing and parenting issues. Marriage is of divine origin.

 **Marriage is still a good idea because it is GOD'S *idea*.**

God Himself instituted and ordained marriage at the very beginning of human history. The second chapter of Genesis describes how God, taking a rib from the side of the man He had already created, fashioned from it a woman to be a "suitable helper" (Gen. 2:20) for the man. Then God brought the man and the woman together and confirmed their relationship as husband and wife, thereby ordaining the institution of marriage.

From the outset, God established marriage as a permanent relationship, the union of two separate people—a man and a woman—into "one flesh." When Adam first laid eyes on Eve he exclaimed, "This is now *bone of my bones* and *flesh of my flesh*; she shall be called 'woman,' for she was taken out of man" (Gen. 2:23, emphasis added). God's design for marriage is found in the very next verse: "For this reason a man will leave his father and mother and be united to his wife, and they will become one flesh" (Gen. 2:24).

"One flesh" is not simply the "gluing" of two people together but rather the "fusion" of two distinct elements into one. If I glue two pieces of wood together, they are bonded but not fused. They remain two separate pieces of wood, and sufficient heat or pressure will break the bond. In the world of chemistry, different elements are linked to each other by chemical bonds that allow them to work together in a particular manner. If that bond is broken, those elements are released and go their separate ways.

It is different with fusion. When two elements are fused into one they become inseparable. A force of sufficient magnitude may *destroy* them, but it can never *disjoin* them. A man and a woman who have become "one flesh" under God's design for marriage cannot be separated without suffering great damage or even destruction. It would be the spiritual equivalent of having an arm or a leg torn from their bodies.

When God ordained that the man and the woman should "become one flesh" He plainly had a permanent, lifelong relationship in mind. Jesus, the great Jewish rabbi and teacher, made this abundantly clear during a discussion with some Pharisees over the question of divorce. The Pharisees asked Jesus if it was lawful for a man to divorce his wife, pointing out that Moses had permitted it in the law.

*"It was because your hearts were hard that Moses wrote you this law," Jesus replied. "But at the beginning of creation God 'made them male and female.' 'For this reason a man will leave his father and mother and be united to his wife, and the two will become one flesh.' So they are no longer two, but one. Therefore what God has joined together, let man not separate"* (Mark 10:5-9).

"What therefore God has joined together, let no man separate." If marriage were of human origin, then human beings would have the right to set it aside whenever they chose to do so. Since God is the one who instituted marriage, He alone has the authority to determine its standards and set its rules. He alone has the authority to do away with it. This He will not do, for the Scriptures are clear: Marriage is a God-ordained institution that involves the joining of a man and a woman as "one flesh" in a lifelong relationship. This institution will last as long as human life lasts on earth. Only in the life to come will marriage be dispensed with.

## *Marriage Is a Foundational Institution*

Another important truth about marriage is that God established it as the first and most fundamental element of human society. While the family is the basic foundation of any healthy society, marriage is the foundation of the family. Marriage is a foundational institution that predates all other institutions. Before there were nations or governments; before there were churches, schools, or businesses; there was the family; and before the family there was marriage.

**While the family is the basic foundation of any healthy society, marriage is the foundation of the family.**

Marriage is foundational because it is on this relationship that God began to build society. When God brought Adam and

Eve together in the garden, marriage was the framework for the development of their social interaction as they grew together. It was in the context of marriage that they learned their responsibilities toward each other and lived out their commitments to each other.

Human society in all its forms depends on marriage for its survival. That is why the current low regard for marriage in the minds of so many is so dangerous. With all traditional values and foundations being assaulted at every turn, is it any surprise that marriage is under attack as well? With so many people so confused about marriage, is it any wonder that society in general is in such disarray? The adversary's global attack on marriage is actually an attack on society itself, and ultimately an attack on God, the creator and manufacturer of society and marriage. The adversary knows that if he can destroy marriage he can destroy families; if he can destroy families he can destroy society; and if he can destroy society he can destroy humanity.

Marriage is also the foundation upon which the Church, the community of believers and God's special society, rests. The New Testament describes the relationship between Christ and His Church as being like that of a bridegroom to his bride. This analogy has significant implications for understanding how husbands and wives are to relate to each other. For example, in his letter to the church in Ephesus the first century Jewish apostle Paul wrote:

*Submit to one another out of reverence for Christ. Wives, submit to your husbands as to the Lord. For the husband is the head of the wife as Christ is the head of the church, His body, of which He is the Savior....Husbands, love your wives, just as Christ loved the church and gave Himself up for her...."For this reason a man will leave his father and mother and be united to his wife, and the two will become one flesh." This is a profound mystery—but I am talking about Christ and the church* (Ephesians 5:21-23,25,31-32).

The relationship between Christ and His Church is a model for that which should exist between husband and wife: a relationship of respect, mutual submission, and sacrificial love.

From Genesis to Revelation the Bible often uses the word *house* to refer to the smallest and most basic unit of society—the family. The "house" is the foundation of society, and marriage is the foundation of the "house." The health of a marriage determines the health of a "house," and the health of a nation's "houses" determines the health of the nation.

 ***A healthy "house" is the key to both a healthy church and a healthy society.***

## Misconceptions of Marriage.

It is the same in the Church. A church's health depends on the health of the "houses" of its members, particularly those in leadership. Good family management is a fundamental requirement for church leaders. Paul made this clear when he wrote to Timothy, "Here is a trustworthy saying: If anyone sets his heart on being an overseer, he desires a noble task" (1 Tim. 3:1). Among other things, "He must manage his own family well and see that his children obey him with proper respect. (If anyone does not know how to manage his own family, how can he take care of God's church?)" (1 Tim. 3:4-5)

A healthy "house" is the key to both a healthy church and a healthy society. The measure of a healthy "house" is a healthy marriage. Marriage is a foundational institution.

## Procreation Is Not the Primary Purpose of Marriage

One misconception many people have, both inside and outside the Church, is that the primary purpose of marriage is the propagation of the human race. The Bible indicates otherwise.

Although in Genesis 1:28 God issued the charge to man to "be fruitful and multiply," and although He defined marriage as the parameters in which reproduction should take place, procreation is not the primary purpose of marriage.

God's command had to do with creation and subduing the created order. "God blessed them and said to them, 'Be fruitful and increase in number; fill the earth and subdue it. Rule over the fish of the sea and the birds of the air and over every living creature that moves on the ground' " (Gen. 1:28). God created man—male and female—and He expected them to procreate and fill the earth with other humans, all of whom would rule over the created order as His vice-regents. Marriage was essentially a *companionship covenant*, the relational structure through which men and women—husbands and wives—would join and become one flesh and *together* rule the earthly dominion God had given them. Procreation is a function of marriage but it is not the main focus.

As contemporary society plainly shows, marriage is not necessary for procreation. Unmarried men and women have no trouble at all making babies. In many parts of the world the number of out-of-wedlock births exceeds the number of babies born to married women. That is one reason why many scientists and sociologists are concerned that at the current rate, within one or two generations the global population will grow beyond the earth's capacity to sustain it.

Contrary to the common idea that marriage is mainly about making babies, marriage actually serves as a deterrent to rampant reproduction. There are at least two reasons for this. First, the social and moral requirement of being married before having children is still very strong in many, many places. Most people are still sensitive to the respectability of marriage, and that respect holds back a lot of procreation that would otherwise take place. Were it not for the institution of marriage, human beings would be even more prolific than they already are. Second, married couples who take their responsibilities seriously are careful not to conceive and give birth to more children than they can adequately love and care for. Paul had some strong words on this subject. "If anyone does not provide for his relatives, and especially for his immediate family, he has denied the faith and is worse than an unbeliever" (1 Tim. 5:8).

There is nothing sinful or unbiblical about careful *advance* family planning. (Let me make it clear that abortion is *not* "family planning," nor is it "health care." Abortion is the termination of life and the premeditated destruction of potential. It is the death of destiny and the interference of divine protocol. Abortion is rebellion against the known will of God.) On the contrary, true family planning is mature, responsible stewardship.

## *Sex Is Not the Primary Purpose of Marriage*

Another common misunderstanding is that marriage exists for the purpose of legitimizing sexual relations. Marriage should never be equated with sex because sex is not the primary purpose of marriage. Sexual union is not and never has been the same thing as marital union. Marriage is a union that implies and involves sexual union as the establishment of a blood covenant, a central obligation, and a pleasure (see 1 Cor. 7:3-5), but the three are not the same.

First of all, marriage involves commitment. Sex has very little to do with commitment; it is a 100-percent physical response to physiological and biochemical stimuli. Sex is one expression of commitment in marriage, but it never creates commitment. By itself, sex neither *makes* nor *breaks* a marriage. Marriage is broader and deeper than sex, and transcends it. Marriage is perhaps one percent sex; the rest is ordinary, everyday life. If you marry for sex, how are you going to handle the other 99 percent?

For many years it has been a common belief that adultery breaks a marriage. That is simply not true. Sex does not create a marriage, so how can it break a marriage? Adultery is sin and, according to the Bible, the only legitimate grounds for divorce for a believer. Even then it is not automatic. Divorce is not mandatory in such instances. Adultery does not break the marriage. Breaking the marriage is a *choice*.

Recognizing that sexual union and marital union are not the same is absolutely essential to any proper understanding of marriage. It is also essential in understanding divorce and remarriage. Marriage is bigger than, distinct from, but inclusive of sexual union. Absence of sexual activity will never unmake a marriage, nor will its presence alone turn a relationship into a marriage. Marriage and sex are related but they are not the same.

## A "Gem" of a Marriage

How then should we define marriage? If marriage is not primarily for sex or procreation, then what is it? As always, we can find the answer in the Bible. God's Word is truly amazing; nothing we read there is there by accident. The basic Greek word for "marry" or "marriage" is *gameo*, which derives from the same root as our English word "gem." That root word literally means to "fuse together." Fusion of different elements into one describes the process by which precious gems are formed deep in the earth. That process is also an apt description of marriage.

Precious gems such as diamonds, rubies, emeralds, and sapphires are formed far underground out of ordinary elements that are subjected to great heat and massive pressure over an extended period of time. Heat, pressure, and time working together can transform even the most common material into something extraordinary. Take coal for example. Coal is formed when partially decomposed wood or other plant matter is combined with moisture in an airless environment under intense heat and pressure. This process does not happen overnight, but requires centuries.

Although coal is basically a form of carbon, its constituent elements can still be distinguished under chemical analysis. Coal that remains in the earth long enough—thousands of years longer—under continuous heat and pressure eventually is transformed into diamond. Chemically, diamond is *pure carbon*. The distinct elements used in its formation can no longer be identified. Pressure has *fused* them into *one* inseparable element. Heat gives diamond its luster.

 **It takes only a few minutes to get married, but building a marriage requires a lifetime.**

Marriage as God designed it is like a precious gem. First of all, it develops over time. Diamonds don't form in ten years; they require millennia. It takes only a few minutes to *get* married, but *building* a marriage requires a lifetime. That's one reason why God established marriage as a permanent, lifelong relationship. There must be sufficient time for two people with separate and distinct backgrounds and personalities to become *fused* together as one flesh.

Secondly, godly marriage becomes stronger under pressure. A diamond is the hardest substance on earth. Millions of tons of pressure over thousands of years fuse and transform carbonized matter into a crystal that can withstand any onslaught. A diamond can be cut only under certain conditions and using specially designed tools. In a similar way, external pressures temper and strengthen a godly marriage, driving a husband and wife closer together. Just as pressure purifies a diamond, so the everyday problems and challenges of life purify a godly marriage. A husband and wife face the pressure together. The harder things get, the stronger their union grows. Marriage fuses two different people into one so that under pressure they become so hard and fast that nothing can break them.

Godly marriages and worldly marriages respond different-ly to pressure. In the world, when the going gets tough, part-ners split up. Like those two pieces of wood glued together, they are bonded but not fused. The heat and pressure of life break them apart. That same heat and pressure fuse a godly couple together so that their marriage grows ever stronger, until they become inseparable and unbreakable.

## Collision of Histories

Marriage is never just the coming together of two people, but a collision of their histories. It is a clash of cultures, expe-riences, memories, and habits. Marriage is the beautiful ac-commodation of another lifetime.

Building a strong marriage takes time, patience, and hard work. One of the hardest adjustments anyone faces is moving from single life to married life. Let's be honest: People do not change overnight. When you marry someone, you marry more than just a person; you "marry" an entire family, a complete history of experiences. That's why it is often so hard at first to understand this person who is now sharing your house and your bed. Both of you bring into your marriage 20 or 30 years of life experiences that color how you see and respond to the world. Most of the time you quickly discover that you see many things quite differently from each other. Difference of viewpoint is one of the biggest sources of stress and conflict in young marriages. Adjusting to these differences is critical to marital survival. Unfortunately, many marriages fail on pre-cisely this point.

All of us filter what we see and hear through the lens of our own experiences. Personal tragedy, physical or sexual abuse, quality of family life when growing up, educational level, faith or lack of faith—any of these affect the way we view the world around us. They help shape our expectations of life and influence how we interpret what other people say or do to us.

None of us enter marriage "clean." To one degree or another, we each bring our own emotional, psychological, and spiritual baggage. Whatever our spouse says, we hear through the filter of our own history and experience. Our spouse hears everything we say the same way. Understanding and adjusting to this requires a lot of time and patience.

Over time and under the pressures of daily life, a husband and wife come to understand each other more and more. They begin to think alike, act alike, and even feel alike. They learn to sense each other's moods and often recognize what is wrong without even asking. Gradually, their personal attitudes and viewpoints shift and move toward each other so that their mentality is no longer "yours" and "mine," but "ours." This is when the gem-like quality of marriage shines most brilliantly. Fusion creates oneness.

A godly marriage is like a precious gem in another way as well. Normally, we don't find gems simply by walking along looking on the surface of the ground as we would searching for seashells on the beach. To find gems, we have to dig deep into the earth and chisel through hard rock. In the same way, we will never obtain God's kind of marriage simply by going along with the crowd, doing what everybody else does. We have to dig deep into the heart of God to discover His principles. Precious gems are rare and so is a genuine marriage. There are no shortcuts, no easy "1-2-3" formulas. We have only God's Word to instruct us and His Spirit to give us understanding and discernment, but that is all we need.

 *We will never obtain God's kind of marriage simply by going along with the crowd, doing what everybody else does. We have to dig deep into the heart of God to discover His principles.*

Rarely will we find anything of true value simply lying on top of the ground. The "good stuff" is most often found deep down where we have to work to get at it. A good marriage is something we have to work at; it doesn't happen by accident. Just as a precious diamond is the final result of a long and intensive process, so is marriage.

So what is marriage? Marriage is a God-ordained institution, a lifelong relationship between one man and one woman. Over time and under the heat and pressure of life, two people under the covenant of marriage come together and are lost in each other to the point where it becomes impossible to tell where one leaves off and the other begins. Marriage is a *process*, a *fusion* of two distinct and different elements into one—a sparkling jewel of love, faithfulness, and commitment that shines brightly in a world of short-lived fads and impermanence.

# PRINCIPLES

1. Marriage is still a good idea because it is God's idea.

2. Marriage is a foundational institution that predates all other institutions.

3. Procreation is not the primary purpose of marriage.

4. Sex is not the primary purpose of marriage.

5. Marriage as God designed it is like a precious gem: a fusing of two different elements into one.

6. Godly marriage develops over time.

7. Godly marriage grows strong under pressure.

8. Godly marriage is a fusion that creates oneness.

## CHAPTER TWO

# *Marriage Is Honorable*

$S$ome time ago during a trip to Germany I had the opportunity to counsel a married couple who were on the verge of divorce. The husband picked me up at the airport, and during the two-and-a-half-hour drive to their home he and I had plenty of time to talk. He began pouring his heart out to me about how much he loved his wife, and yet nothing seemed to be working out right. Continual pressure and friction in their relationship had brought them to the point of being ready to call it quits. Things had gotten so bad that they were not even sleeping in the same bed. This troubled husband could not understand what had gone wrong between him and his wife. He was begging me for some answers. I told him that I couldn't talk to him by himself because two people are involved in marriage. I would have to talk to the two of them together.

It was very late when we arrived at the house, but instead of going to bed the three of us sat down and began to talk. By the time we finished, it was 4:00 am. As they unfolded to me the troubles they were facing, I shared with them the most basic cause of marital failure, which is when people do not understand that marriage itself is honorable, more so than those who are involved in it.

 *Success in marriage does not depend on spouses committing themselves to **EACH OTHER** as much as it does to their committing themselves to **MARRIAGE**, the unchanging institution that they have **MUTUALLY** entered into.*

Marriage is a steady, unchanging institution entered into by two people who are constantly changing as they grow and mature. Those changes can be unnerving and frustrating and can easily ignite conflict. Respect for the honorableness and stability of marriage can give a husband and wife a solid anchor that enables them to weather the storms of change as they grow toward oneness. Recognizing the unchanging nature of marriage as an institution can encourage them during times of conflict to seek alternatives to ending their marriage. Success in marriage does not depend on spouses committing themselves to *each other* as much as it does to their committing themselves to *marriage*, the unchanging institution that they have *mutually* entered into.

## It's Not Who You Love, but What You Love

The Bible presents marriage as an institution that should be highly respected and esteemed above all other institutions. Hebrews 13:4 says, "Marriage should be honored by all, and the marriage bed kept pure, for God will judge the adulterer and all the sexually immoral." The King James Version reads, "Marriage is honorable in all..." "Honorable" translates the Greek word *timios*, which also means "valuable, costly, honored, esteemed, beloved, and precious." *All* means "all": The Greek word is *pas*, meaning "all, any, every, the whole, thoroughly, whatsoever, and whosoever." Marriage, then, should be valued and esteemed, and held in highest honor at all times in all things by all people everywhere. That is God's design.

Notice that the verse says, "*Marriage* should be honored by all"; it says nothing at all about the people *in* the marriage. A common notion with most people is that the parties in a marriage—the husband and wife—should honor each other and hold each other in high esteem. This is certainly true, but ultimately it is not what makes a marriage work. What is more important is that they honor and esteem *marriage itself*. Let's face it, none of us are lovable all the time. There are times when we say something hateful or do something foolish, leaving our spouse hurt or angry. Maybe he or she has done the same to us. Either way, holding our marriage in high honor and esteem will carry us over those bumpy times when one or the other of us is unlovable or difficult to honor.

One of the keys to a long and happy marriage is understanding that it's not *who* you love, but *what* you love that's important. Let me explain. Consider an average couple; we'll call them John and Sarah. John and Sarah meet at a party and begin talking. John is 22, handsome, dark-headed, athletic, and has a good-paying job. Sarah is 20, attractive, intelligent, has beautiful hair, and also has a good job. Attracted to each other right off the bat, John and Sarah start going out together. Their relationship continues to grow until one night John says, "Sarah, I love you," and Sarah replies, "I love you, too, John."

Since John and Sarah have fallen in love, they decide to get married. John gives Sarah a ring and they begin planning their wedding. John and Sarah are so happy in their love that they feel it will sustain them forever. Somewhere along the way, however, they both had better figure out *what* they love about each other, or they are headed for trouble in their marriage.

John needs to ask himself, "Why do I love Sarah? What is there about her that causes me to love her? Do I love her because of *who* she is, or for some other reason? Do I love her because of her attractive figure or her beautiful hair or her good job?" Sarah at 20 is all of those things, but what about when she is 40? What if at 40 Sarah has put on some weight and lost her slim figure because she has borne three or four children? What if she no longer has that good job because she stayed home to raise those children? If John loves all of the things Sarah is when she is 20, how will he feel about her when she is 40?

Sarah needs to ask herself the same questions about John. At 22, John may be everything Sarah has dreamed about in a man, but what about when he is 42 and has started losing his hair? What if he has lost much of his youthful athletic build because he has worked in an office day after day for 20 years? What if the company he worked for went bankrupt and the only job he has been able to find is as a mason's helper making half the amount of money he did before?

It is not enough just to know *who* we love; we need to know *what* we love. We need to know *why* we love the person we love. This is critically important for building a happy and successful marriage.

 *The person we marry is not the person we will live with, because that person is changing all the time.*

The point I am trying to make is this: The person we marry is not the person we will live with, because that person is changing all the time. Today, my wife is not the same woman I married, nor am I the same man she married. Both of us have changed in many ways and continue to change every day. If we who are constantly changing trust solely in each other to keep our marriage going, we are in real trouble. No matter how much we love, honor, and esteem each other, that alone might not be enough in the long run. Respecting and esteeming the honorability of marriage as an unchanging institution helps bring stability to our ever-changing relationship.

The person we marry is not the person we will live with. That is why marriage itself is to be honored and esteemed more than the people who are in it. People change, but marriage is constant. We must love marriage more than our spouse.

## *Marriage Is Bigger Than the Two People in It*

If marriage itself is to be honored and esteemed even above the people involved in it, what does that mean in practical terms? For purposes of illustration it may help to compare marriage to working at a job. Let's imagine that you and I go to work for the same company. The company is a form of institution, and we have joined that institution by accepting employment there. We have committed ourselves to the *institution*.

Suppose we end up working side by side at adjacent desks. We build a good working relationship and get along fine for awhile. Then, one day we have a sharp disagreement over something and exchange heated words. We both decide that we are not talking to each other anymore.

What happens next? Do we quit our jobs simply because we had a falling out? I hope not. (Some people quit over this kind of thing, but it is almost always a sign of immaturity.) No, instead we both go home, still angry and at odds, but the next day there we are again, back at our desks. Why? Because we are committed to the *institution* more than we are to the people *in* the institution. A week passes, and even though we still are not talking, there we are, continuing to work side by side. There may be conflict between us, but we are both still committed to the institution.

Another week passes, and one day you suddenly ask, "Could I borrow your eraser?" and I say, "Okay." Slowly, our disagreement is passing and we are starting to communicate again. Before many more days go by we're talking and laughing like old friends, going to lunch together, and everything is back to normal. We make up after our disagreement because we regard the institution as more important than our personal feelings. This kind of thing happens all the time in institutions. People have conflict, but eventually reconcile their differences because the institution is bigger than their conflict.

This truth is a key to properly understanding marriage. The institution of marriage is more important than our personal feelings. There will be times when we will not be in agreement with our spouse, but that has nothing to do with the marriage. We must never confuse our personal feelings or conflicts with the institution of marriage. Marriage is honorable, respectable, and unchanging, while we at times are dishonorable or unrespectable, and we are always changing. Marriage is perfect, while we are imperfect.

Commitment to the marriage, rather than commitment to the person, is the key to success. No matter what my wife says or does to me, I'm hanging in there, and I know that regardless of what I do, she will still be there. We are committed to our marriage even more than we are committed to each other. When we disagree or argue or have other conflict, we work it out because it is only temporary. We don't break up the institution over it, because the institution is bigger than we are.

When you have a conflict with a fellow employee on your job, you work it out for the sake of the institution—the company—which is bigger than both of you. Since you have to work together you might as well solve your problem. The same attitude should apply in marriage. When a husband and wife are in conflict, they should come together and agree, "Sure, we have our differences, and we're always changing, but this marriage is bigger than both of us. We're in it for the long haul, so let's make up. Let's do whatever we need to do to make this thing work."

Marriage is bigger than the two people in it, which is the way it should be. God instituted marriage; it belongs to Him, not us. *Marriage is two imperfect people committing themselves to a perfect institution, by making perfect vows from imperfect lips before a perfect God.*

## A Perfect Vow and Imperfect Lips

A vow is different from a promise. A promise is a pledge to do or not do a specific thing, such as a father promising to take his son to the zoo. A vow, on the other hand, is a solemn assertion that binds the vow maker to a certain action, service, or condition, such as a vow of poverty. As I wrote in my earlier book, *Single, Married, Separated, and Life After Divorce:*

A promise is a commitment to do something later, and a vow is a binding commitment to begin doing something now and to continue to do it for the duration of the vow. Some vows, or contracts, are for life; others are for limited periods of time.[1]

God takes vows very seriously:

A vow is unto death, which is why God said, "Don't make it if you are not going to keep it"....

"Unto death" does not mean "until your natural death." It means giving God the right to allow you to die if you break the vow. Under the Old Covenant, if they broke vows and God's mercy did not intervene, something serious happened.

A vow is not made to another person. Vows are made to God or before God; in other words, with God as a witness.[2]

God's attitude toward vows is revealed plainly in the Scriptures. "When you make a vow to God, do not delay in fulfilling it. He has no pleasure in fools; fulfill your vow. It is better not to vow than to make a vow and not fulfill it" (Eccles. 5:4-5).

Marriage is a vow and breaking that vow is a serious matter because it also breaks one's fellowship with God. The old testament prophet Malachi expressed God's perspective on faithfulness to the marriage vow in the following words:

*Another thing you do: You flood the Lord's altar with tears. You weep and wail because He no longer pays attention to your offerings or accepts them with pleasure from your hands. You ask, "Why?" It is because the Lord is acting as the witness between you and the wife of your youth, because you have broken faith with her, though she is your partner, the wife of your marriage covenant* (Malachi 2:13-14).

 **Marriage is bigger than the two people in it.**

*Because marriage is a perfect vow made before a perfect God by two imperfect people, only God can make it work.* Don't expect perfection from your spouse. **Marriage** *is perfect, but* **people** *are imperfect.* If you don't believe that, just take a look in the mirror. The institution of marriage is constant; it never changes. People change all the time. If you want success in your marriage, commit yourself to that which does not change. Commit yourself to the institution of marriage. It will become your center of gravity and help keep you solid.

## Changing Institutions Is Not the Answer

Once we understand that marriage is an institution to be respected and esteemed, the thought of divorce never enters our minds. Respect for the institution of marriage helps carry us through those times when either our spouse or we act in an unrespectable manner. We don't abandon the institution because of conflicts or problems that arise.

One of the problems that many people in our society have is a tendency to move frequently from job to job, quitting whenever something does not go their way. Not only is this a sign of immaturity and of an unwillingness to resolve issues, it quickly erodes their credibility in the eyes of potential employers. Consider this: You go in for a job interview and they ask you, "Where did you last work?" After you answer, they ask, "Why did you leave?" The purpose of these questions is to assess your credibility. This employer wants to know what kind of person you are and whether or not you will be an asset to the company.

Suppose you answer, "I left because I didn't like my boss," or "I left because of problems I had with some fellow workers." Don't be surprised if this employer does not hire you. Why should he think that you would be any different working for him? If he finds out that you have had ten jobs over the last three years, he certainly won't hire you. He doesn't want to become number eleven on your list.

Changing institutions is not the solution to the problem. The key to growth and maturity is to hang on during the tough times and work through the problems. This is just as true in marriage as it is on the job. When problems arise in a marriage relationship, a lot of people think that their problems will go away if they simply divorce and then marry someone else. This is simply not the case. Marital difficulties are almost *never* one-sided. If you bail out of the marriage before resolving the issues, then whatever problems *you* brought into that relationship you will carry into the next one. They may take a different shape, but they will be the same problems.

 *Changing institutions is not the solution to the problem. The key to growth and maturity is to hang on during the tough times and work through the problems.*

There was a time not too many years ago when traditional views of marriage and the family were held in highest honor and respect in western society. Divorce was virtually unheard of and, when it occurred, carried a heavy social stigma. Not anymore. Biblical concepts of marriage and the family have come under strong attack over the past couple of generations.

The humanistic philosophies so prevalent today have helped remove the social and moral stigma from divorce. As a result, divorce and remarriage have become not only commonplace, but also acceptable, even in the eyes of many believers. Some people have even gone so far as to suggest that the measure of one's manhood or womanhood is determined by how many different sex partners they have. That concept is completely twisted. It is sick and satanic, yet reflects what is currently happening in our society.

Because of the pervasiveness of worldly philosophies regarding marriage and family, many believers are ignorant of God's standards. We need to look again at the words of Jesus when He said, "But at the beginning of creation God 'made them male and female.' 'For this reason a man will leave his father and mother and be united to his wife, and the two will become one flesh.' So they are no longer two, but one. Therefore what God has joined together, let man not separate" (Mk. 10:6-9).

These verses reveal two important truths to understand about God's kind of marriage. First, God will join together only that which He can allow. God cannot and will not sanction sin in any form. Can you imagine God taking two sinners, joining them together, and blessing them? To do so would be to bless and encourage sin. At "the beginning of creation," when God brought them together, Adam and Eve were pure and holy, unsullied and uncorrupted by sin. Prior to the fall, their marriage was the model of everything God intended. God cannot and will not bless a sinful relationship. No God-sanctioned union can possibly exist between unbelievers or between anyone who "marries" with unresolved sin in their lives or who come together under circumstances that are sinful or otherwise contrary to God's standards.

The second truth in Mark 10:6-9 is that what God *has* joined together, man must not separate. Human civil government possesses neither the authority nor the power to disjoin a God-ordained marriage between two believers. In the natural, "civil" marriages established by civil law may also be disestablished by civil law. People who get married outside of God can also get unmarried outside of God. In the spiritual, marriage that God has sanctioned cannot be broken by the decree of men. This raises an important question. *If believers come to the marriage altar for God to join them together, why then do so many of them go to the court to get "un-joined"?*

Human courts have no power to separate what God has joined. God-style marriage is a fusion, not a bonding. What God has joined, He alone can put asunder. He won't do it, however, because to do so would violate His own standards. For believers, changing institutions is not the answer.

## A Successful Marriage Depends on Knowledge

*Knowledge* is the answer. A successful marriage has little to do with love. Love does not guarantee success in marriage. Love is very important for *happiness* in marriage, but by itself it cannot make a marriage work. The only thing that makes a marriage work is knowledge. As a matter of fact, the only thing that makes *anything* work is knowledge. Success depends on how much we *know* about something, not how we *feel* about it.

Most married people love and feel good about each other, but many do not know how to communicate effectively or relate well to each other. There is a huge difference between recognizing feelings and knowing how to deal with conflict. Some people define intelligence as the ability to solve complex problems. More accurately, intelligence is the ability to face reality and deal with problems while maintaining one's sanity. Dealing with problems is not necessarily the same as solving them. Some problems can't be solved. An intelligent person is someone who can maintain his stability and sense of self-worth under any circumstances, evaluate the situation, deal effectively with the problem, and come out intact on the other side.

There is a great need today for intelligence and knowledge regarding marriage to offset widespread ignorance on the subject. Even the Christian Church, which should be the voice of authority on the subject of marriage, is suffering because many believers, including leaders, are biblically illiterate where marriage and the family are concerned. In this day when all the old values are being challenged left and right, both within and without the Church, many people are confused, uncertain of what to believe anymore. The root cause of this confusion is lack of knowledge.

Knowledge is critical for success and survival in anything. In Hosea 4:6a God says, "My people are destroyed from lack of knowledge." "My people" refers to the children of God. Even Christians need knowledge. The greatest knowledge of all is to know God. Proverbs 1:7 says, "The fear of the Lord is the *beginning* of knowledge, but fools despise wisdom and discipline" (emphasis added). It doesn't matter how often we come to church or how often we worship the Lord; without knowledge, we have no guarantee of success.

One of the things that really bothered me as a young Christian was hearing about so many other Christians getting divorced. If followers of Christ were failing in their marriages, what hope was there for anybody else? Here were people who supposedly were filled with the Holy Spirit, who supposedly knew the Holy God, and yet they couldn't seem to live together and get along. If that was true, we might as well forget the whole thing!

It took me a little while to learn that success in marriage depends on more than just being saved. It takes more than just being in love. Being a believer and being in love are both important in marriage, but they carry no automatic guarantee of marital success. We need knowledge of biblical principles; the design parameters that God Himself established. Biblical principles never change. The principles for a successful marriage and family that God gave Adam and Eve still work today. They are universally applicable in every age and in every culture. Trouble comes when we violate or ignore those principles.

Ultimately, marriage will not survive on love alone, or on feelings. By itself, just being born again is not enough to guarantee success. *A successful marriage hinges on knowledge—knowing and understanding God's principles.*

 **God designed marriage for success, and only His counsel can make it successful.**

Marriage is honorable. God instituted marriage, and He alone has the right to dictate its terms. The institution of marriage is subject to the rules, regulations, and conditions that God has set down, and He has revealed them in His Word.

God designed marriage for success, and only His counsel can make it successful. No one is better at making something work than the person who designed it. It would be a mistake to use Toyota parts to repair your Ford automobile. Toyota parts are designed for Toyotas, not Fords. Instead, you should take your Ford automobile to a licensed Ford service dealer. No one knows Ford cars better than the Ford Motor Company. Would you take your Mercedes-Benz to a Ford dealer for repairs? Not if you're smart. Only a Mercedes dealer could guarantee to repair it properly. Guaranteed success means using the right "service man." It means referring back to the designer.

Marriage is the same way. Success in marriage means using the right "service man" or "authorized dealer"—referring back to the designer for guidance. No one knows a product like the manufacturer. No one understands marriage better than God does. He created it, He established it, He ordained it, and He blesses it. Only He can make it work. Marriage is honorable because it is of divine rather than human origin. If we want *our* marriage to be honorable and successful, we must know, understand, and follow the principles that God has set out in His "manual," the Bible. That is the only sure corrective for the ignorance and misinformation that characterizes so much of the world's view of marriage.

# PRINCIPLES

1. Marriage is a steady, unchanging institution entered into by two people who are constantly changing as they grow and mature.

2. The institution of marriage is more important than our personal feelings.

3. Commitment to the marriage, rather than commitment to the person, is the key to success.

4. Marriage is two imperfect people committing themselves to a perfect institution, by making perfect vows from imperfect lips.

5. God will join together only that which He can allow.

6. What God *has* joined together, man must not separate.

7. Success depends on how much we *know* about something, not how we *feel* about it.

8. A successful marriage hinges on knowledge—knowing and understanding God's principles.

## Endnotes

1. Myles Munroe, *Single, Married, Separated, and Life After Divorce*. (Shippensburg: Destiny Image Publishers, Inc., 1992) p. 91.

2. Ibid.

## ↶ CHAPTER THREE ↷

# Why Get Married, Anyway?

People get married for lots of reasons, some good, others not so good. Many marriages today fail because the couple does not understand either the purpose or the principles of successful marriage. They lack *knowledge*. Modern society's confusion about marriage results in many couples' marrying for the wrong reasons—reasons that are insufficient for sustaining a healthy, lifelong relationship.

No one should ever get married without first carefully and clearly answering the question, "Why?" Deliberate and thoughtful consideration in advance will prevent a lot of problems, heartache, and regret later on. Knowing why you want to marry can confirm you in a good decision and help you avoid making a bad decision.

Because knowledge is critical to success, it is important first of all to recognize some of the most common *unhealthy* reasons people use in choosing to get married. I have listed ten. This list is based not on guesswork but on evidence drawn from studies of countless failed marriages. We are not talking fiction here, but real life.

## Ten Unhealthy Reasons for Getting Married

### 1. To spite parents.

Believe it or not, some people get married in order to spite or get back at their parents. "I'm so sick and tired of having to do everything they tell me! I'll show them! I don't have to stay around here anymore!" They may resent their parents' rules or chafe under their parents' discipline. They may be angry over their parents' disapproval of their friends, particularly that special boyfriend or girlfriend. That anger or resentment may drive them to do something foolish, like getting married without thinking it through. Even though they may know nothing about marriage, they jump at the chance because they see it as a quick way to get out from under their parents' restrictions.

Marrying to spite one's parents is a crazy reason to get married. That marriage is headed for trouble right away. The overriding emotion is negative—anger, resentment, bitterness—and not conducive for a healthy long-term relationship. Qualities essential to success, such as love, commitment, and faithfulness, are either absent or take a secondary role behind the primary motivation of spite. A person who marries out of spite sees his or her spouse not as a lover, companion, and friend, as much as a means of escape from dominating parents. That is insufficient grounds upon which to build a happy and successful marriage.

### 2. To escape an unhappy home.

This is similar to the first unhealthy reason. Some people grow up in unhappy or difficult home situations, and all they want to do is escape. There may be physical, verbal, or sexual abuse involved. One or both parents may be addicted to alcohol or drugs. Home life may be a constant litany of anger, shouting, cursing, and quarreling. Whatever the reason, some young people are dying to get away from home, and often see marriage as their way out. This is extremely foolish and unwise. The desire to escape an unhappy home life is no reason to get married. If you simply *must* get away, then go out and find a job, get an apartment, and move out on your own. People who marry in order to escape rarely find what they are looking for. In the end, they simply exchange one kind of unhappiness for another.

### 3. A negative self-image.

Unfortunately, some people get married in the hope that it will make them feel worthwhile and give meaning to their life. Their self-image is so low that they constantly need someone else to affirm their worth and tell them that they are all right. A marriage begun on this basis is in trouble before it even gets rolling.

A spouse who enters marriage with a negative self-image comes into that relationship as only half a person. If *both* people have self-image problems, they are really in for a rough time. A healthy marriage brings two wholes together, not two halves, forming a union that is greater than the sum of its parts. Two people who come together and who are confident of their own self-worth and comfortable in their personal identities can build a happy, successful, and meaningful marriage.

Marriage will not solve the problem of a negative self-image. Marriage magnifies the defects in our character and exposes our self-concept. It will only make it worse. We all must find our sense of self-worth in our relationship with Christ, in our identity as beloved children of God and heirs to His Kingdom: precious souls created in God's image for whom Jesus died. Truly understanding that we are members of the "royal family" will affect how we think, feel, and act. That is the cure for a negative self-image.

### 4. Marrying on the rebound.

This reason is closely related to the last one. People who have been hurt in a former relationship or marriage often feel discouraged and depressed, with their self-esteem lying in the dirt. They are quick to jump headlong into a new relationship with the first person who comes along offering sympathy or concern. By this they hope not only to ease their hurt but prove to themselves that there is nothing wrong with them. You don't have to get married to prove that you are all right; there are other ways to do that. It gets back to the self-image issue. If you're okay, you're okay; marriage won't change that one way or the other.

The problem with marrying on the rebound is that it is not a marriage of love, but of convenience. You're hurting and doubting yourself, and along comes someone who sympathizes with you and shows compassion. Both of you may mistake this for true love and make a quick decision to get married. In reality, however, no love is involved. For you it is only a marriage of convenience, a "quick and easy" way out of your dilemma. Don't fall for it. A "rebound" marriage is destined for trouble.

### 5. Fear of being left out.

This fear affects both men and women, but tends to hit women harder than men, particularly as they get older. Even in our modern society, a woman's sense of worth is linked to marriage, home, and family more so than is a man's. Many women start to get worried if they reach the age of 30 and still are not married. Sometimes panic sets in. "What am I going to do? Everybody's getting married except me! All of my friends are married. I'm the only one out of my graduating class who isn't married. What's wrong with me?"

With this mindset, some women will grab the first guy who comes along and shows any interest in her. He may not be any good for her, but that doesn't matter. He may be a defective character destined to be a deficit to her life, but she doesn't see that. She's desperate! All she sees is that he is interested in her. Even if he is only taking advantage of her, she convinces herself that he loves her and that she loves him. When he pops the question, she says, "Thank God!" and accepts eagerly. The only problem is that God had nothing to do with it. Her panic and fear of becoming an "old maid" have pushed her into a bad decision.

Men make the same mistake. Fearing the thought of being a bachelor all their lives, some men marry women who are not right for them. Fear of being left out causes many men and women to settle for a marriage that is less than what they could have had if they had been patient and trusted God.

When a person marries out of fear of being left out, one of two things usually happens. Either the marriage breaks up, or they "grin and bear it," too embarrassed to admit to the world, and especially to their friends and family, that they made a mistake. Either way, the happiness they sought eludes them, and all they know is sorrow instead.

### 6. Fear of independence.

Some people grow up so dependent on their parents that when they become adults, and face the prospect of being out on their own, they get married in order to have someone else to depend on. Many times the parents bear the responsibility for their children's dependency. Whether deliberately or not, they insist on doing everything for their children, never teaching them how to think or act for themselves. Some parents have a tendency to always think of their children as "my baby," and try to hold onto them forever.

Children who grow up dependent on their parents often enter marriage expecting their spouse to take care of them and provide the same security they have always known. The first time they have to stand up and be independent, they crumble, because they never learned how. Once they are faced with the necessity of handling responsibilities they never had to worry about before, some of them can't deal with it.

No one who is afraid of independence is ready to get married. Successful marriage requires that both husband and wife be comfortable and capable with independence.

### 7. Fear of hurting the other person.

This happens more often than we would like to admit. Let's say a young man and a young woman have been dating for awhile. She begins to talk marriage but he isn't so sure. Even though he realizes that he does not love her and knows that marriage is not the answer, he's afraid of what will happen if he breaks up with her. Maybe she has said more than once, "If you leave me, I'll just die!" or even more ominously, "If you ever leave me, I'll kill myself!" Since he doesn't know how to let her down easily and doesn't want to hurt her, he offers to marry her. These roles could just as easily be reversed, with the man putting pressure on his girlfriend who isn't sure what to do.

One reason this problem crops up is because some people do not understand the different levels of friendship. Just because a guy takes a girl out for ice cream does not mean they are ready to get married. They are just friends. Everything might be fine until one or the other of them gets carried away and starts reading more into their relationship than is really there. That person starts applying pressure until the other one begins to feel guilty and obligated.

No marriage stands a chance if it is based on fear of any kind. Don't get married simply because you are afraid of hurting the other person. It is much better for both of you to go through temporary pain now than to get married and set yourselves up for a lifetime of pain.

### 8. To be a therapist or a counselor for the other person.

It may sound crazy, but this is why some people get married. They feel a sense of responsibility for someone who needs the benefit of their wisdom, counsel, and advice. Be careful. Don't get carried away. Men, just because a young lady comes to you for counsel doesn't mean you should marry her. Ladies, just because a young man may seek out your advice doesn't mean he should become your husband. Marriage is not the proper forum for therapy. There are other avenues.

It is not at all uncommon for people in long-term therapy to develop romantic feelings toward their therapist. Insecure people are drawn easily to those they regard as authority figures, or even as surrogate parents. Professional counselors have to watch out for this kind of thing all the time.

*A healthy marriage is the joining of a man and a woman as equal partners, both of whom are emotionally mature and secure in their self-image and personal identity.*

A healthy marriage is the joining of a man and a woman as equal partners, both of whom are emotionally mature and secure in their self-image and personal identity. If you marry someone who is always looking to you as a counselor, you will never get any rest and they will drain you emotionally. Insecure in his or her own abilities and lacking self-confidence, your spouse will consult you about any and every little thing. Nothing will wear you out faster than a spouse who cannot think for himself or herself, or who will not make any independent decisions. Don't get caught in that trap. No one who needs continual counseling is ready for marriage.

**9. Because of having sex.**
There is an old teaching that says that a man and a woman who have sex are married in fact if not in law. This is simply not true. We have already seen that sex does not equate to marriage. Sex alone neither makes nor breaks a marriage. According to God's design, sex is appropriate only within the bounds of marriage. It enhances and enriches a marriage that has already been established on other proper foundations. Outside of marriage, sex is inappropriate and psychologically damaging, emotionally dangerous, and sinful. Having sex, therefore, is not a reason to get married; it is a reason to repent. Sexual abstinence is the only appropriate behavior for unmarried people, and especially believers.

*Sexual abstinence is the only appropriate behavior for unmarried people, and especially believers.*

**10. Because of pregnancy.**
Becoming pregnant is no more of a reason for getting married than having sex. The age of the "shotgun wedding" is

long past. Still, there are some people who feel that even though sex alone is not reason enough for marriage, pregnancy changes things. Without a doubt it raises certain ethical, moral, and legal issues, particularly for the father of the child. Even so, the fact of pregnancy alone is insufficient grounds for marriage. On the surface, a pregnancy is evidence only of sexual activity. It does not necessarily indicate the existence of love or commitment between the man and woman who conceived the child. Compounding the sin and mistake of an out-of-wedlock pregnancy with the mistake of a bad marriage is foolish and unwise. It will lead inevitably to heartache and pain for everyone involved, and especially for the innocent child caught in the middle of it all.

One mistake won't put you out of the race for life. Many people who have conceived and borne children out-of-wedlock later go into happy marriages. Like sex, pregnancy alone is not a reason to get married, but a reason to *repent*. Even if you never marry the person with whom you conceived the child, God can give the two of you the grace and wisdom to behave responsibly for the health and welfare of that child.

## *Ten Healthy Reasons for Getting Married*

Now that we have identified some common unhealthy reasons for marriage, we need to examine some healthy reasons. The ten that follow should not be regarded as separate entities, but as part of a greater whole. While each of these is a good reason for getting married, none of them *alone* are sufficient. A healthy, successful, and godly marriage will embrace most, but not necessarily all, of these reasons.

### 1. Because it is God's will.

This is perhaps the most important reason of all. God designed marriage, and no one knows it better than He does. As believers, our top priority should be to discern and obey God's will in *all things*. This includes our choice of a mate. For some reason, whether it is due to lack of knowledge or lack of faith, many believers have difficulty trusting God with this area of their lives. A couple who is considering marriage needs to take plenty of time to pray together, seeking God's will in the matter. Just because you are both believers doesn't automatically mean that you are right for each other for marriage. Be patient. Trust God and honestly and humbly seek His will and wisdom. If He is calling you to marry, He wants to join you to someone with whom you can build a strong, godly home filled with love and grace—a home that exalts Jesus Christ as Lord and a harmony in vision and purpose. If you seek His counsel, He will bring the right person into your life, and you will know it when He does.

*If God is calling you to marry, He wants to join you to someone with whom you can build a strong, godly home filled with love and grace—a home that exalts Jesus Christ as Lord.*

## 2. Expressing God's love to the other person.

Marriage is a physical picture of the spiritual union and love that exist among the Father, the Son, and the Holy Spirit. It also depicts the love of God for His people and Christ's love for His Church. Divine love, or *agape*, is primal love, the original and highest love from which all other forms of love derive. *Agape* is a *choice*, an act of the will. By His very nature, God *chooses* to love us even though we have nothing within ourselves to commend us in that love. Paul, the great early church leader and missionary, wrote, "But God demonstrates His own love for us in this: While we were still sinners, Christ died for us" (Rom. 5:8). God's love is unconditional love.

Properly expressed, human love in all its forms takes its pattern from the divine agape that issues forth from the Father. Since *agape* is the love that God displays toward all people, a person does not have to be married to experience it.

However, marriage does provide a wonderful avenue through which a man and a woman can express this godly love to each other in a uniquely personal way. *Agape* is one of the catalysts for the "fusion" that characterizes true marriage. When a husband and wife *choose* to love each other unconditionally, that choice will carry them through the times when they are unlovable. A successful and healthy marriage always begins with *agape*. Other forms of love grow out of and build upon the firm foundation of God's love.

 *Properly expressed, human love in all its forms takes its pattern from the divine agape that issues forth from the Father.*

### 3. Expressing personal love for the other person.

Healthy marital love involves the proper blending of the various types and degrees of love. First is *agape*, the unconditional love of God that gives birth to all other forms. Marriage should also be an expression of personal love between the husband and wife, a desire to show a level of esteem and regard toward each other that they show toward no one else. Marital love includes the element of *phileo*, a Greek concept of love best understood as "tender affection." Husbands and wives should be tender and affectionate toward each other. A marriage relationship is also characterized by *eros*, which is physical, or sexual love. These expressions of personal love are healthy reasons for marriage, but they need to be properly founded on the unconditional *agape* love that comes from God.

### 4. To fulfill sexual needs and desires in a godly way.

Sexual desire is God-given and, in its proper place, healthy and good. By itself, the desire for sex is a poor and shallow reason for getting married. In conjunction with other reasons, however, such as love and the desire for companionship, the desire for sexual fulfillment is a strong and natural motivation. Love that produces in a man and a woman the desire to commit themselves to a lifelong relationship also generates the desire to express that love sexually. Believers who are serious about their commitment to Christ will seek to fulfill their sexual needs and desires in a godly way. Marriage is the God-ordained vehicle for fulfilling God-given sexual desire. Paul's words to the believers in Corinth provide wise and practical counsel on the matter:

> *Now for the matters you wrote about: It is good for a man not to marry. But since there is so much immorality, each man should have his own wife, and each woman her own husband.* **The husband should fulfill his marital duty to his wife, and likewise the wife to her husband.** *The wife's body does not belong to her alone but also to her husband. In the same way, the husband's body does not belong to him alone but also to his wife.* **Do not deprive each other except by mutual consent** *and for a time, so that you may devote yourselves to prayer. Then come together again so that satan will not tempt you because of your lack of self-control.... Now to the unmarried and the widows I say: It is good for them to stay unmarried, as I am.* **But if they cannot control themselves, they should marry, for it is better to marry than to burn with passion** (1 Corinthians 7:1-5, 8-9, emphasis added).

*Marriage is the God-ordained vehicle for fulfilling God-given sexual desire.*

### 5. The desire to begin a family.

The desire to have children is a godly desire, but it is neither a primary nor even a necessary reason for marriage. There are many happily married couples who have no children, either by choice or otherwise. Marital happiness and success do not depend on the presence of children. Children are a wonderful blessing and enhance a marriage, and those couples who desire children desire a good thing. Psalm 127:3-5 says, "Sons are a heritage from the Lord, children a reward from Him. Like arrows in the hands of a warrior are sons born in one's youth. Blessed is the man whose quiver is full of them. They will not be put to shame when they contend with their enemies in the gate." There is no better environment in which to raise children than in a Christian home anchored by a strong Christian marriage.

### 6. Companionship.

The desire for companionship is a worthy reason for getting married. Everyone has a built-in need for a "bosom buddy," an intimate friend or companion. Although such companionship and friendship can be found outside of marriage, the companionship forged between a husband and wife is particularly rich and rewarding. Humans are social beings, created to enjoy and thrive on each other's company. When God created the first man, He found no "suitable helper" for him among all the other creatures.

 *A husband should be his wife's best friend and companion, and a wife, her husband's.*

*So the Lord God caused the man to fall into a deep sleep; and while he was sleeping, He took one of the man's ribs and closed up the place with flesh. Then the Lord God made a woman from the rib He had taken out of the man, and He brought her to the man. The man said, "This is now bone of my bones and flesh of my flesh; she shall be called 'woman,' for she was taken out of man." For this reason a man will leave his father and mother and be united to his wife, and they will become one flesh* (Genesis 2:21-24).

A husband should be his wife's best friend and companion, and a wife, her husband's. Marriage is designed for companionship.

**7. To share all things together with the other person.**

There is a lot of truth in the old saying that when we share our sorrow, our sorrow is halved, and when we share our joy, our joy is doubled. Sorrow and difficult times in our lives are easier to bear when we have a soul mate to share them with. Our joy and laughter multiply when we have a bosom companion who joins in. Godly love that draws a man and a woman together creates in them a desire to share all things with each other, especially the ongoing daily adventure of life itself. Marriage is designed for the man and woman who have decided that they wish to spend the rest of their lives together in a relationship of mutual love, respect, and sharing.

**8. To work together to fulfill each other's needs.**

Marital love also stirs up in a husband and wife the desire to meet each other's needs. This is a give-and-take process that requires much sensitivity on the part of both. Every person is born with ongoing physical, mental, emotional, and spiritual needs. There is the need for food, water, clothing, and shelter; the need for security and peace of mind; the need to be free from fear; the need for aesthetic enrichment; the need for peace with God and intimate fellowship with Him. Marriage is a tailor-made opportunity for a man and woman to work together to fulfill their legitimate needs. Together, and with steadfast trust in the Lord, they can meet any challenge and overcome any obstacle. "Though one may be overpowered, two can defend themselves. A cord of three strands is not quickly broken" (Eccles. 4:12).

**9. To maximize each person's potential.**

The key to a successful life is to die empty—to maximize your potential by learning to think and act beyond your self-imposed limitations. In a successful marriage, both partners are committed to helping each other reach their full potential. The desire to help the person you love the most to become all he or she can be is a healthy motivation for marriage. The bounds of the marital union provide an ideal environment in which husbands and wives can strive to express their fullest personal, spiritual, and professional potential. In partnership together they can encourage one another, lift up one another, pray for one another, defend one another, challenge one another, comfort one another, and affirm one another.

 *The bounds of the marital union provide an ideal environment in which husbands and wives can strive to express their fullest personal, spiritual, and professional potential.*

### 10. Enhancement of spiritual growth.

Because it comes from God, marriage is designed for believers: men and women who walk by faith and not by sight and live in a daily and growing personal love relationship with Jesus Christ. Both husband and wife together should continually encourage each other to grow in the Lord. They should worship together, pray together, read and discuss the Scriptures together, and hold each other accountable for their spiritual walk with Christ. Structurally, "the husband is the head of the wife as Christ is the head of the church" (Eph. 5:23a). By his leadership and submission to Christ, the husband is to set the tone and direction for the spiritual growth of the family, but both husband and wife bear a mutual responsibility for the spiritual health of their marriage. Any couple who is serious about building a godly marriage will make enhancing each other's spiritual growth a very high priority.

\* \* \* \* \*

One common characteristic of all ten *unhealthy* reasons for marriage is that they are essentially *self-centered*. Selfishness is never a healthy quality on which to try to build a marriage. In contrast, the ten *healthy* reasons are fundamentally *unselfish*. Based as they are on God's nature of unselfish love, they are *self-giving* reasons that focus on the needs and welfare of the other person. This is a critical distinction that can make the difference between success and failure, between happiness and unhappiness, and between a good marriage and a bad marriage.

## PRINCIPLES

1.  A healthy marriage brings two wholes together, not two halves, forming a union that is greater than the sum of its parts.

2.  We all must find our sense of self-worth in our relationship with Christ; in our identity as beloved children of God and heirs to His Kingdom, precious souls created in God's image for whom Jesus died.

3.  Ten healthy reasons for marriage:

    *   God's will

    *   Expressing God's love to the other person

    *   Expressing personal love for the other person

    *   To fulfill sexual needs and desires in a godly way

    *   The desire to begin a family

    *   Companionship

    *   To share all things together with the other person

    *   To work together to fulfill each other's needs

    *   To maximize each person's potential

    *   Enhancement of spiritual growth

4.  Because it comes from God, marriage is designed for believers: men and women who walk by faith and not by sight and live in a daily and growing personal love relationship with Jesus Christ.

## CHAPTER FOUR

# Everyone Should Have a Garden Wedding

The world's first wedding took place in the Garden of Eden. There God ordained and sanctified the marriage of the man and woman whom He had created. Chapters 1 and 2 of Genesis depict marriage in its ideal state as God designed it, where Adam and Eve enjoyed a relationship characterized by peace, harmony, and equality, along with continual, unbroken fellowship with their Creator. Genesis chapter 3 presents a starkly different picture: Sin has shattered the harmony of the human couple's relationship with each other and destroyed their fellowship with God. Chapters 1 and 2 portray marriage "inside the garden," while chapter 3 shows marriage "outside the garden." The only place to experience God's marriage is "inside the garden." Any marriage "outside the garden" is not God's marriage.

Genesis chapters 1 and 2 picture marriage before the Fall, as God designed it. Chapter 3 reveals what marriage became after the Fall, as the world corrupted it. In practical terms this means that none of the conditions, blessings, or promises that attend the "inside the garden" marriage of chapters 1 and 2 are guaranteed for the "outside the garden" marriage of chapter 3. Inside the garden Adam and Eve enjoy mutual love, respect, and equality; outside the garden they make excuses, blame each other, and lie to God about each other. Inside the garden they share the same spirit, the Spirit of God; outside the garden that Spirit has departed and they are like strangers to each other. Inside the garden they are united in spirit *and* in flesh; outside the garden all they have is flesh.

God's standard of marriage is based on the garden's qualification. No one can truthfully claim that God has joined them who do not come to the marriage altar in the context of the garden. Because it is designed for believers, true marriage is not a union of spirits as much as a union of flesh. In the Garden of Eden, there was no need for Adam and Eve to be married in spirit because they already shared the same spirit. Their spirits were already *fused*. In the flesh, however, they were separate people. Their marriage "inside the garden" was to unite them physically—to *fuse* them into "one flesh," just as they were already "one spirit."

Every day, thousands of couples around the world get married assuming that God has joined them together. In most cases this simply is not true because they have not married within the garden context. They do not share the same spirit because either one or both of them have never been born again of the Spirit of God. Because of this, they have no guarantee of success, no safeguard against the destructive forces that would pull them apart.

God's promises in Scripture apply to all who believe and obey Him—everyone who is called a child of God and who shares His Spirit. No one who is outside the Spirit of God has any guarantee of receiving His promises. Where marriage is concerned, success or failure may depend in large measure on whether or not that marriage exists within the garden context.

 *Even though they are born again, many believers have trouble in their marriages because they have unknowingly embraced the world's values and views rather than God's.*

Knowledge is a critical key to success in anything, and marriage is no exception. Even Spirit-filled believers may fail in marriage unless they know and understand the fundamental differences between marriage "inside the garden" and marriage "outside the garden." Even though they are born again, many believers have trouble in their marriages because they have unknowingly embraced the world's values and views rather than God's. They need to learn how to look to the Holy Spirit for the wisdom and knowledge to bring their marriage "inside the garden."

## *Equal Authority, Equal Dominion*

The first two chapters of Genesis contain important clues to help us understand what marriage was meant to be and the relationship that should exist between husband and wife. On the sixth and final day of creation, after the heavens and the earth were in place and the earth teemed with plant, animal, and sea life, God put the climax on His creative activity by creating man. Mankind—male and female—was the apex, the crowning glory of God's creativity. He had a special place and plan for these, the greatest of His creations.

> *Then God said, "Let Us make man in Our image, in Our likeness, and let **them** rule over the fish of the sea and the birds of the air, over the livestock, over all the earth, and over all the creatures that move along the ground." So God created man in His own image, in the image of God He created him; **male and female He created them**. God blessed **them** and said to **them**, "Be fruitful and increase in number; fill the earth and subdue it. Rule over the fish of the sea and the birds of the air and over every living creature that moves on the ground"* (Genesis 1:26-28, emphasis added).

Notice that the authority to rule over the created order and to fill and subdue the earth was given to the man and woman *together*. Male and female *both* were created in God's image, each designed to perfectly complete and enhance the other. *Both* were endowed with the capacity and the authority to rule over the physical realm as God's vice-regents. Note also that their authority to rule extended over all of God's lesser creatures—fish, birds, and land animals—but *not* over each other. According to God's original design, man and woman were to exercise *equal* authority and *equal* dominion.

God's command to subdue and rule applied equally to both the man and the woman. In the Garden of Eden, Adam and Eve possessed the same spirit, acted with the same authority, and exercised the same power. They had dominion over "every living creature that moves on the ground." This included the serpent. Genesis chapter 3 makes it clear that satan, that fallen angel, the tempter and accuser, was present in the garden, in the form of a serpent. Because Adam and Eve represented the highest of God's creation, and because satan was in their realm, he was under their jurisdiction. Adam and Eve possessed both the authority and the power to subdue the devil. Their failure to do so led to disaster.

 *In the garden Adam and Eve were equal in personhood and authority.*

The second chapter of Genesis also reveals that in the garden Adam and Eve were equal in personhood and authority. Genesis 2:18-24 describes how God made Eve from one of Adam's ribs to be a "suitable helper" for him, someone who would be perfectly and completely compatible with him physically. The Hebrew word for "rib" can also be translated as "side." Eve was formed from part of Adam's side. She was of the same "stuff" as Adam: the same spirit, the same mind, the same essence, and the same divine image. She was bone of his bone and flesh of his flesh, in every essential and fundamental way his equal. An ancient Hebrew proverb found in the Talmud, the authoritative collection of Jewish tradition, says, "God did not create woman from man's head, that he should command her, nor from his feet, that she should be his slave, but rather from his side, that she should be near his heart."

 *One in spirit and one in flesh, the man and woman in the garden exercised equal power and authority, ruling together the physical, earthly domain that God had given them.*

One in spirit and one in flesh, the man and woman in the garden exercised equal power and authority, ruling together the physical, earthly domain that God had given them.

## Male Headship Is Based on Knowledge

Equality of personhood, power, and authority does not mean that there was no priority of leadership in the garden between Adam and Eve. One thing that Genesis chapter 2 makes clear is that God positioned the man as head of the family unit. In God's design, headship in marriage is the man's responsibility. As soon as God placed Adam in the Garden of Eden, He established the parameters under which the man would live and work.

*The Lord God took the man and put him in the Garden of Eden to work it and take care of it. And the Lord God commanded the man, "You are free to eat from any tree in the garden; but you must not eat from the tree of the knowledge of good and evil, for when you eat of it you will surely die"* (Genesis 2:15-17).

Being responsible for caring for the garden gave Adam fruitful and productive work to do. At the same time, God gave him free reign throughout his environment. The only restriction on

Adam's freedom was God's prohibition against eating from the tree of the knowledge of good and evil.

It is important to note that Adam received these instructions before Eve came on the scene. Because he was created first, Adam was privy to information from God that Eve did not have. It was Adam's responsibility to pass along this information to his wife. As "head" of the unit, Adam was the covering for his family. That covering was based on his responsibility.

Why was Adam made the head of the family? Was it because he was physically stronger? No. Today it is commonly known that men and women are essentially equal in physical strength, but in different ways. Generally, men are stronger from the waist up while women are stronger from the waist down. A woman's body is specifically designed for bearing the physical stress and pressure of childbirth. Very few men could handle that kind of pain. Adam's position of headship was not due to physical strength.

Was it his physical appearance? I don't think so. Physically, women in general are more attractive than men. Someone once said tongue-in-cheek that because the man was made first, he was the "rough copy" while the woman was the more refined end product.

Was Adam smarter? No. Men and women have the same intellectual capacity. Was Adam more spiritual? No. Adam and Eve shared the same spirit.

It appears that Adam's headship was as much a matter of timing as anything else. Adam was head because he was created first and possessed information that Eve did not have. Adam's headship was based on *knowledge*. This fact has serious implications for understanding what headship means. The husband is the head of his wife (see Eph. 5:23) but this does *not* mean that he rules over her as her boss. *Headship is not rulership; it is **leadership***. As head, the man is to provide spiritual leadership and direction to the family. He is supposed to chart the course. His spiritual temperature should set the climate for his entire house.

 *Headship is not rulership; it is leadership.*

Many marriages today, including Christian marriages, suffer because the husbands do not properly understand or carry out their responsibilities as the head of their families. Too often their headship degenerates into an authoritarian rule that dominates both wife and children. Sometimes they abdicate their leadership entirely so that the headship falls to their wives, at least in practice if not in name.

When both husband and wife are clear on the issue of headship, that understanding will promote marital harmony and success. The husband decides where the family is going, while the wife decides how they are going to get there. The husband provides direction; the wife, maintenance. Where a husband goes has a lot to do with what his wife does, and what a wife does has a lot to do with where her husband goes. Both are necessary and both work together. Direction is the first step, and action is the second step.

In his headship, Adam had vital information from God upon which Eve's security and welfare depended. He bore the responsibility for instructing her on God's command regarding the tree of the knowledge of good and evil. The man's headship, therefore, is based on *knowledge* and primarily involves teaching and instructing his family in the ways of God and all spiritual matters in general.

## Leaving the Garden

In the beauty of the Garden of Eden Adam and Eve exercised dominion over the created order, enjoyed full marital bliss and harmony, and engaged in unbroken fellowship with their Creator. These idyllic conditions were shattered by the subtle and crafty schemes of the adversary. Appearing in the guise of a serpent, this archenemy of God set his sights on destroying the purity, innocence, and order of life in the garden. The woman was his target, and doubt was his weapon.

> *Now the serpent was more crafty than any of the wild animals the Lord God had made. He said to the woman, "Did God really say, 'You must not eat from any tree in the garden'?" The woman said to the serpent, "We may eat fruit from the trees in the garden, but God did say, 'You must not eat fruit from the tree that is in the middle of the garden, and you must not touch it, or you will die.'" "You will not surely die," the serpent said to the woman. "For God knows that when you eat of it your eyes will be opened, and you will be like God, knowing good and evil." When the woman saw that the fruit of the tree was good for food and pleasing to the eye, and also desirable for gaining wisdom, she took some and ate it. She also gave some to her husband, who was with her, and he ate it. Then the eyes of both of them were opened, and they realized they were naked; so they sewed fig leaves together and made coverings for themselves* (Genesis 3:1-7).

Because Eve expressed no surprise when the serpent spoke to her, it is reasonable to conclude that this probably was not their first conversation. In her innocence regarding the knowledge of good and evil, Eve had no reason to distrust the serpent's words or to suspect him of trickery. His question was very subtle, skillfully sowing in her mind a seed of doubt regarding God's integrity: "Did God *really* say, 'You must not eat from any tree in the garden'?" (emphasis added) This is the way the adversary operates. God's archenemy, identified in the Judeo-Christian Scriptures as the devil, or satan, seeks to undermine God's character in people's minds through innuendo and doubt and by twisting the truth.

*One of the adversary's primary tactics is to make us doubt who we are.*

Eve's response to the serpent's question reveals that Adam had fulfilled his responsibility to inform her of God's command regarding the tree of the knowledge of good and evil. When she said that to eat from the tree or touch it meant death, the serpent flatly contradicted God: "You will not surely die, [but] your eyes will be opened, and you will be like God, knowing good and evil." One of the adversary's primary tactics is to make us doubt who we are. In whose image and likeness were Adam and Eve created? *God's.* They did not need to eat the fruit of the tree of the knowledge of good and evil in order to become like God; *they were already like Him!*

The seed of doubt grew in Eve's mind until she was confused about who she was and about what God had said. In her confusion, and because the fruit of the tree looked appealing, she decided to eat it. Where was Adam while all of this was going on? According to verse 6 he was *with her*, at least at the time she ate the fruit, because she gave some to him and he ate also. The passage does not tell us where he was during Eve's conversation with the serpent. Although there is no break in the narrative, Eve's decision to eat the fruit did not necessarily occur immediately afterward. Some time may have passed while her doubt grew and the temptation got stronger.

It appears that Adam was not around when Eve and the serpent talked. By his absence, Adam failed in his responsibility to protect and cover his wife. Although they both possessed the authority to rule over the serpent, they surrendered that authority by listening to him, and he gained control over them. Eve was deceived, but Adam sinned with his eyes wide open. The "knowledge" they received for all their trouble was awareness that they had sinned and that God's Spirit had departed from them. Suddenly, they were estranged from each other as well as from God. The "honeymoon" was over. By their disobedience to God, their marriage moved "outside the garden."

## Adam, Where Are You?

After Adam and Eve disobeyed God in the garden, He confronted them with their sin, and the way He did it reveals an important truth about His design for marriage.

> *Then the man and his wife heard the sound of the Lord God as He was walking in the garden in the cool of the day, and they hid from the Lord God among the trees of the garden. But the Lord God called to the man, "Where are you?" He answered, "I heard You in the garden, and I was afraid because I was naked; so I hid." And He said, "Who told you that you were naked? Have you eaten from the tree that I commanded you not to eat from?" The man said, "The woman You put here with me—she gave me some fruit from the tree, and I ate it." Then the Lord God said to the woman, "What is this you have done?" The woman said, "The serpent deceived me, and I ate"* (Genesis 3:8-13).

Notice that although it was Eve who listened to the serpent, who was deceived by him, and who first took the forbidden fruit and ate it, when God confronted them He sought out *Adam*. "But the Lord God called to *the man*, 'Where are you?'" This was not a question of location but of disposition. God already knew where Adam was and what he had done. The intent of His question was to get Adam to acknowledge his sin and take responsibility for his actions. The Lord was saying to Adam, "How did you get in the state you are in? You have fallen and My Spirit has left you. There is no longer any fellowship between you and Me. How did you get into this position?"

If Eve was the instigator, the first to disobey by eating the forbidden fruit, why then did God seek out Adam? There are at least two reasons. For one thing, even though Eve sinned first, Adam was just as guilty because he also ate the fruit. He could have refused, but he did not. More importantly, however, God came to Adam because, as head of the family, Adam was responsible. Adam bore the responsibility not only for telling his wife what God said, which he apparently had done, but also for watching over her and guarding her. He was supposed to be her covering. Where was he during his wife's encounter with the adversary? Because he was not where he was supposed to be, or doing what he was supposed to be doing, Adam bore direct responsibility for their failure.

 *Fear and separation are not part of God's plan or desire for us.*

Adam's response to the Lord's question makes it clear that some fundamental changes had occurred in their relationship. "I heard You in the garden, and I was afraid because I was naked; so I hid." When a person loses fellowship with God, several significant things happen. First, their sense of separation from God causes them to run from Him. Adam hid himself. Second, they become fearful. Adam was afraid. Until he disobeyed God he had never known fear. Now fear dogged his every step.

 *Love and fear cannot coexist. Where love abounds, fear is banished; where fear rises, love diminishes.*

Fear and separation are not part of God's plan or desire for us. He created us to love Him and to enjoy permanent fellowship with Him. Fear is a foreign element in that relationship. It interferes with the free expression of love. In his second letter to Timothy, his young protégé, Paul, the great missionary and teacher of the first century wrote, "For God did not give us a spirit of timidity, but a spirit of power, of love and of self-discipline" (2 Tim. 1:7). Another word for timidity is *fear*. John, a writer of the New Testament and one of Jesus' special disciples, wrote, "God is love. Whoever lives in love lives in God, and God in him….There is no fear in love. But perfect love drives out fear, because fear has to do with punishment. The one who fears is not made perfect in love" (1 Jn. 4:16b, 18).

Love and fear cannot coexist. Where love abounds, fear is banished; where fear rises, love diminishes. Because of their sin, Adam and Eve forfeited the love, peace, harmony, and fellowship they had enjoyed with the Lord and with each other, and found that guilt and fear had replaced them. This change affected every area of their lives, including their marriage. A marriage without love is a slave to fear and division. Such are the common characteristics of marriage "outside the garden."

 *A marriage without love is a slave to fear and division.*

## Playing the Blame Game

Another sign of the fundamental change that sin brought to their relationship is that Adam and Eve began playing the blame game. Blame flourishes where love is absent. Adam blamed Eve, Eve blamed the serpent, and neither was willing to accept personal responsibility for their actions. People often say and do ridiculous things when they try to avoid taking responsibility. Consider what Adam said: "The woman You put here with me—she gave me some fruit from the tree, and I ate it." He makes it sound as though he was completely helpless. In effect, Adam is telling God, "It's her fault, this woman that *You* gave me. She body-slammed me, got me in a headlock, tore my mouth open, stuffed the fruit in, and moved my jaws up and down saying, 'Come on, chew it.' "

*Blame flourishes where love is absent.*

Simply stated, Adam did not want to take responsibility for what happened to his family. Neither did Eve. When God asked, "What is this you have done?" she tried to pass the buck. "The serpent deceived me, and I ate." On the surface, what she said is true; the serpent *did* deceive her. That did not excuse her from responsibility, however. She knew what God had said and chose to disobey.

Reluctance to assume responsibility is a very common problem in our modern society, a symptom of the sinfulness of a human race in rebellion against our Creator. "Pop" psychology tells us that we are all "victims." If we're messed up it is because of our environment, or because we were abused as children, or we were socially or economically deprived, or any number of other excuses. We bear no responsibility for our actions or for how we turned out. No matter what happens, it is always someone else's fault—our husband, our wife, our children, our boss—anyone except ourselves.

This same attitude characterizes marriage "outside the garden." When no one is willing to accept responsibility, everybody suffers. People can become downright illogical when they want to avoid responsibility. In an effort to justify irresponsible behavior they start using excuses that don't make any sense and state them as if they are irrefutable law. The world's design for marriage is the opposite of God's design. Marriage "outside the garden" is the marriage of blame, irresponsible activity, transferring and passing the buck, and men failing to take their rightful and responsible place as head of the home. In the world's system, marriage can be jettisoned when the going gets rough.

One additional characteristic of marriage "outside the garden" is husbands exercising authoritarian rule over their wives. This is a consequence of Eve's sin. God said to her, "I will greatly increase your pains in childbearing; with pain you will give birth to children. Your desire will be for your husband, and *he will rule over you*" (Gen. 3:16, emphasis added). It is important to note that this is not part of God's original design for the husband and wife relationship, but a description of the situation that now exists because of sin.

 ***The husband bears overall responsibility for the health and welfare of his wife and family, but he is not the "boss."***

In God's kind of marriage, the husband does not *rule* his wife but exercises *headship*. He gives leadership and direction and they rule together. The husband bears overall responsibility for the health and welfare of his wife and family, but he is not the "boss." As head of the family he leads the family, not as a tyrant or dictator, but with love, grace, wisdom, and knowledge under the lordship of Christ.

# PRINCIPLES

1.  According to God's original design, man and woman were to exercise *equal* authority and *equal* dominion.

2.  In God's design, headship in marriage is the man's responsibility.

3.  Headship is not rulership; it is *leadership*.

4.  The man's headship is based on *knowledge* and primarily involves teaching and instructing his family in the ways of God and all spiritual matters in general.

5.  Marriage "outside the garden" is the marriage of blame, irresponsible activity, transferring and passing the buck, and men failing to take their rightful and responsible place as head of the home.

6.  As head of the family, the husband leads the family, not as a tyrant or dictator, but with love, grace, wisdom, and knowledge under the lordship of Christ.

⋐ CHAPTER FIVE ⋑

# A Happy Marriage Is No Accident

$\mathcal{A}$ happy marriage is no accident. As with every other area of life, success in marriage does not happen automatically. The secret to success in any endeavor is *planning*, and successful planning depends on *knowledge*. It is only when we have accurate and adequate information that we can plan for success.

Many of us are willing to spend years in school receiving an education that we believe will prepare us for success in our chosen career or profession. We pursue education because education makes us versatile, and versatility increases our marketability. Increased marketability enhances the likelihood of our success. Rather than leave our success to chance, we plan carefully for it.

There was a time when a person entering the labor force at age 18 or 21 spent his or her entire working life with the same employer. Today it is not at all uncommon for workers to change jobs or employers four or five times or more during their careers. The fact that frequent career changes have become the norm in modern society makes education and knowledge even more important to success.

If we are so careful about planning for career success, why aren't we just as careful about planning for success in marriage? After all, we spend years preparing for a career that may change at any time, yet devote very little time preparing for a relationship that is supposed to last a lifetime. If we are not careful we can end up spending too much time preparing for the wrong things. There is nothing wrong with going to school and getting an education or deliberately planning for success in meeting career goals. The problem is that there are many people who have successful careers but failed marriages because they spent much time learning how to get along with their boss and no time learning how to get along with their spouse. We invest more in preparation to make a living than to live life effectively.

As with any other endeavor in life, success in marriage depends on information and planning. Marriage is an investment, and success is directly proportional to the amount of knowledge and time invested in it. Success is not a gift, but the result of careful and deliberate preparation. Success is directly related to investment: when you invest in time and passion, you will more-likely succeed.

No one who hopes to build a new house approaches the project haphazardly. Success in such a venture means buying the right piece of property, securing the services of a qualified architect, and making certain that sufficient financing is available to bring the whole project to completion. It is important to plan for the *end* before beginning, to count the cost up front, and try to anticipate the pitfalls and difficulties that will occur along the way.

Jesus emphasized the importance of this kind of advance planning when He said, "Suppose one of you wants to build a tower. Will he not first sit down and estimate the cost to see if he has enough money to complete it? For if he lays the foundation and is not able to finish it, everyone who sees it will ridicule him, saying, 'This fellow began to build and was not able to finish' " (Lk. 14:28-30). Although Jesus was speaking here specifically of counting the cost of following Him as a disciple, His words provide wise counsel for us with regard to any endeavor we undertake. We must *plan* for success. We must give the same attention to building a home as we do to building the house. Many beautiful houses are not homes.

## Knowledge and Revelation

Marriage is no different. The same principle applies. A happy marriage cannot be left to chance. Just like building a house, a successful marriage is the product of careful planning and deliberate design, the right material, good advice, and qualified contractors.

Many believers make the mistake of assuming that because they know the Lord and have the Holy Spirit they are guaranteed success in marriage. Proverbs 1:7 says, "The fear of the Lord is the beginning of knowledge, but fools despise wisdom and discipline." Fear of the Lord is the *starting place* of knowledge. No matter how smart we are or how educated, until we know the Lord we have no true knowledge. That is where we must begin.

 *We must become students of the Word of God, fluent in the spiritual principles that govern life.*

One of the ministries of the Holy Spirit in our lives is to bring us into the knowledge of the truth. Jesus said, "But the Counselor, the Holy Spirit, whom the Father will send in My name, will *teach you* all things and will *remind you* of everything I have said to you" (Jn. 14:26, emphasis added). The Holy Spirit cannot teach us if we will not sit down to learn, and He cannot remind us of something we never learned to begin with. We must become students of the Word of God, fluent in the spiritual principles that govern life. Only then can the Holy Spirit teach us and remind us.

When it comes to marriage, we have no guarantee of success if we do not know the principles of success. We cannot expect the Spirit of God to "remind" us of principles or truths we never learned in the first place. If we never learn how to communicate with our spouse, if we never learn how to relate properly or how to deal with conflict, the Holy Spirit has nothing of which to "remind" us. That is why knowledge is so important. At the same time, knowledge by itself is not enough. Knowledge alone can lead us to wrong conclusions. When illuminated by the Holy Spirit, knowledge becomes revelation. We need the wisdom of the Spirit to enable us to properly understand and apply our knowledge.

## *Knowledge Overcomes Marital Illiteracy*

One of the biggest challenges facing couples today, whether married or unmarried, is marital illiteracy. Many marriages fail or otherwise fall short of reaching their full potential because the couples never learn what marriage is really all about. What understanding they do have is either very shallow, or shaped by the philosophy of the world rather than by the principles of God, or both. Likelihood of success increases greatly when the misconceptions of ignorance are dispelled by the light of truth and knowledge.

The marriage relationship is a school, a learning environment in which both partners can grow and develop over time. Marriage does not demand perfection but it must be given priority. It is an institution peopled exclusively by sinners, and finds its greatest glory when those sinners see it as God's way of leading them through His ultimate curriculum of love and righteousness.

 ***Marriage is a learning environment in which both partners can grow and develop over time.***

Marriage has the potential of expressing God's love to its fullest possible degree on earth. The will of the couple is the critical factor. A marriage relationship will express God's love only as far as both partners are willing to allow the Lord to really work in and through them. This is a totally unselfish love where the husband and wife "submit to one another out of reverence for Christ" (Eph. 5:21); where the wife respects her husband (v. 33) and submits to him "as to the Lord" (v. 22); and where the husband loves his wife as himself (v. 33), "just as Christ loved the church and gave Himself up for her" (v. 25). When two totally different people come together and live and work as one, giving unselfishly of themselves and loving, forgiving, understanding, and bearing with each other, outside observers will see at least a little bit of what the love of God is all about.

 *Marriage is one of the refining processes by which God shapes men and women into the people He wants them to be.*

A Christian marriage is the total commitment of a husband and wife to each other and individually to the person of Jesus Christ, a commitment that holds nothing back in either the natural or the spiritual realm. It is a pledge of mutual fidelity, a partnership of mutual subordination. Marriage is one of the refining processes by which God shapes men and women into the people He wants them to be.

## Building on a Firm Foundation

Anything of a lasting nature is built on a firm and solid foundation, and marriage is no different. The only sure foundation for life is the Word of God. In one of His most famous teachings, Jesus vividly illustrated the danger of trying to build a life on an inadequate foundation.

*Therefore everyone who hears these words of Mine and puts them into practice is like a wise man who built his house on the rock. The rain came down, the streams rose, and the winds blew and beat against that house; yet it did not fall, because it had its foundation on the rock. But everyone who hears these words of Mine and does not put them into practice is like a foolish man who built his house on sand. The rain came down, the streams rose, and the winds blew and beat against that house, and it fell with a great crash* (Matthew 7:24-27).

Just as a house built on a poor foundation will be blown away in a storm, so a marriage is unlikely to survive the tempests of life unless it is firmly established on bedrock spiritual principles. Let's consider ten foundation stones upon which to build a happy and successful marriage.

**1. Love.**

Love can be described in many different ways, but we are concerned here with agape, the love that defines the very nature of God. Agape is self-denying and self-giving, sacrificial love of the type that Paul, one of the writers of the New Testament, spoke of when he wrote:

*Love is patient, love is kind. It does not envy, it does not boast, it is not proud. It is not rude, it is not self-seeking, it is not easily angered, it keeps no record of wrongs. Love does not delight in evil but rejoices with the truth. It always protects, always trusts, always hopes, always perseveres. Love never fails* (1 Corinthians 13:4-8a).

Love in marriage is more than just a feeling or an emotion; it is a *choice*. Love is a decision you make anew every day with regard to your spouse. Whenever you rise up in the morning or lie down at night or go through the affairs of the day, you are choosing continually to love that man or that woman you married.

**Love in marriage is more than just a feeling or an emotion; it is a CHOICE.**

Understanding that love is a choice will help keep you out of trouble when temptation comes (and it will). Knowing you have made a decision to love your husband or your wife will carry you through those times when he or she has made you angry, or when you see that handsome or attractive coworker at the office. You could have married someone else, but that's not the point. The point is, you made a decision. When you married your spouse, you chose to love and cherish him or her for the rest of your life. That love must be freshened daily.

One of the most important foundation stones for a happy marriage is a sacrificial love for your spouse that you choose to renew daily.

### 2. Truth.

Truth is fundamental in marriage. A marriage that is not based on truth is headed for trouble right away. The greatest and most reliable source of truth is the Bible, which is the Word of God, who is Himself truth and the one who designed and instituted marriage. Every conscientious husband and wife should measure their marriage by the unchanging standard of the principles found in God's Word. The Bible is a truthful and reliable guide for every area of life.

*Every conscientious husband and wife should measure their marriage by the unchanging standard of the principles found in God's Word.*

Truthfulness between husband and wife is an indispensable part of a successful marriage. No one's interests are served if spouses are not honest with each other. Honesty, tempered and seasoned with love, fosters an environment of trust.

### 3. Trust.

Trust is closely related to truth. If a husband and wife want their marriage to be happy and successful, they must be able to trust each other implicitly. Nothing damages a marriage more than broken trust. It's hard to grow and prosper in an atmosphere of bitterness, resentment, and suspicion. That is why both partners should take great care to ensure that they do not say or do anything to give each other any reason to doubt or distrust them. Trust enables a husband and wife to enjoy a relationship characterized by openness and transparency, with no secrets or "locked rooms" that are kept off limits to each other. Trust is also an essential element of commitment.

 *Nothing damages a marriage more than broken trust.*

### 4. Commitment.

Commitment is a frightening word to many people in our society today. They are afraid of being locked in or tied down to any kind of a long-term arrangement. That is one reason why many marriages do not last. A man and a woman approach the marriage altar and exchange their vows but are just going through the motions, giving only lip service to commitment. Their idea of marriage is to hang together until the going gets rough, and then they can split. If their marriage "works," okay, and if it doesn't, oh well. Few people who marry *plan* for their marriages to fail, but neither do they specifically *plan* for success. Those who do not plan for success are virtually guaranteed to fail.

Commitment is the lifeblood of marriage. Part of our problem is that we do not understand the nature of a covenant. Marriage is a "blood covenant" of sorts and, like the blood covenants of old, it lasts a lifetime. A blood covenant was neither entered into nor broken lightly. Violation of a blood covenant brought serious consequences. Marriage involves just as serious a commitment. It is first of all a commitment to the institution of marriage and, second, an exclusive commitment to that person we have chosen to love and cherish for life.

*Commitment is the lifeblood of marriage.*

### 5. Respect.

Any healthy relationship, marriage included, must be built on mutual respect. To respect someone means to esteem that person, to consider him or her worthy of high regard. Wives should respect their husbands and husbands should respect their wives. One reason why so many marriages are in trouble is because the husband has never learned to regard his wife with proper respect. Many men grow up to regard women as little more than sex objects to be possessed and used at will. Never learning any different, they carry this same ignorant viewpoint into marriage.

 *Whoever **desires** respect **must** show respect to others and live in a manner worthy of respect.*

God created man—male and female—in His own image. He created them equal in every significant way. Husbands and wives who see each other as made in God's image will never have any problems with respect. Whoever *desires* respect must *show* respect to others and live in a manner worthy of respect. Anyone who would be respected must be respectable.

### 6. Submission.

Healthy marriages are built not only on mutual respect but also on mutual submission. We hear so often that wives are supposed to submit to their husbands that we forget that submission goes both ways. "Submit to one another out of reverence for Christ. Wives, submit to your husbands as to the Lord....Husbands, love your wives, just as Christ loved the church and gave Himself up for her" (Eph. 5:21-22,25). Jesus' giving Himself up in death out of love for His Church was the ultimate act of submission. Ephesians 5:25 says that husbands are supposed to love their wives in that same way, a love characterized by sacrificial, self-giving submission.

 *Submission is the willingness to give up our right to ourselves, to freely surrender our insistence on having our own way all the time.*

Properly understood, there is nothing demeaning about submission. It is chosen freely, not imposed from without. Essentially, submission is the willingness to give up our right to ourselves, to freely surrender our insistence on having our own way all the time. Submission means putting the needs, rights, and welfare of another person ahead of our own. A marriage built on this kind of submission will grow healthy, strong, and fulfilling.

### 7. Knowledge.

It would be almost impossible to over-emphasize the importance of knowledge as a firm foundation for marriage. Many marriages struggle or fail because of lack of knowledge. Couples enter married life with no clue as to what marriage is or is not. They carry unrealistic and unreasonable expectations of themselves, their spouses, and their relationship as a whole.

 *With all the resources that are currently available, and because so much is at stake, there is no excuse today for marital ignorance or illiteracy.*

This is why a period of courtship and engagement is so important and why premarital counseling is indispensable. Couples considering marriage need time to get to know one another. They need time to talk about their dreams, their desires, and their expectations. They need time to study and learn the spiritual foundations and principles for marriage that God has given in His Word. With all the resources that are currently available, and because so much is at stake, there is no excuse today for marital ignorance or illiteracy.

### 8. Faithfulness.

Faithfulness is closely related to commitment and also has a lot to do with trust. When we speak of faithfulness in marriage, we most often have sexual relations in mind. Faithful partners will be true, reserving sexual expression exclusively for each other. This is why many married couples who were sexually active before marriage often have trouble in their relationships. The basic element of faithfulness is missing. Even if they have pledged to be faithful to each other, there is always that shadow of doubt. It doesn't take much for that shadow to become a dark storm cloud looming over everything.

*Marital fidelity means that your spouse's health, happiness, security, and welfare take a higher place in your life than anything else except your own relationship with the Lord.*

Marital faithfulness involves more than just sexual fidelity. Being faithful to your wife also means defending her and affirming her beauty, intelligence, and integrity at all times, particularly before other people. Faithfulness to your husband means sticking up for him, always building him up and never tearing him down. Marital fidelity means that your spouse's health, happiness, security, and welfare take a higher place in your life than anything else except your own relationship with the Lord.

### 9. Patience.

Patience is another essential foundation stone for building a successful and happy marriage. Why? Marriage brings together two totally different people with different experiences, different backgrounds, different temperaments, different likes and dislikes, and sometimes even different cultures. Because of these differences, both partners will have to make major adjustments in their lives and attitudes if their marriage is to succeed. Some bumps and bruises along the way are inevitable. She may wear her hair in a way he doesn't like. He may drive her up the wall with his habit of leaving his dirty clothes lying around everywhere. They may have conflict regarding expectations, money management, use of leisure time, sex, parenting—any number of things. The critical key in dealing with conflict and adjusting to differences is patience. Both partners will need truckloads of it!

 *The critical key in dealing with conflict and adjusting to differences is patience.*

### 10. Financial stability.

Financial stability is one of the most often overlooked foundation stones of marriage. Many young couples who are planning to marry give little thought to the importance of entering marriage with a well-established financial base. I cannot count the number of times I have seen this for myself. A young couple comes to me and says, "We would like to get married."

"Are either of you working?"

"No."

"Then how do you expect to make it?"

"We're in love. We'll make it. Love will find a way."

Love is certainly important, even critical, but let's be practical. Love won't pay the rent or put food on the table. Adjusting to married life is difficult and challenging enough on its own. The last thing a couple needs is to go into the marriage with a lot of minuses. Financial instability is one of the biggest minuses of all. If you're having money problems *before* you are married, what makes you think they will go away *after* you are married?

The time to think about finances is *before* the wedding—long before. A couple should discuss the matter frankly and honestly and have a clear financial plan in place before they take their vows. There should be a steady and dependable source of income. At the very least, the man should have steady employment. No woman, even if she has her own career and plans to continue working, should marry a man who does not have a job. If she does, she will most likely end up supporting him, rather than the other way around.

Financial difficulty is one of the main causes of marital failure. *Never* underestimate the importance of financial stability to a successful marriage.

> *Financial difficulty is one of the main causes of marital failure.*

## Checking Your "Marriage Ability" Traits

In addition to these foundation stones, there are several "marriage ability" traits we should consider—qualities of personality and character that will enhance the building of a strong marriage. Check these out and see where you stand. I have listed eight.

**1. Adaptability.** This is simply the ability to adapt to changing conditions. No matter how carefully we prepare for marriage, we cannot predict everything. Unexpected situations will pop up with annoying frequency, forcing us to change our plans. Just the fact of two completely different people coming together as one will inevitably call for flexibility. Be adaptable. Expect the unexpected. Consider it as an opportunity to grow, to move in a direction you might never have thought of otherwise.

**2. Empathy.** This is sensitivity to the needs, hurts, and desires of others—the ability to feel with them and experience the world from their perspective. A lot of conflict and misunderstanding between spouses could be avoided if they would simply try to increase their ability to empathize with each other, to walk in each other's shoes for awhile.

**3. Ability to work through problems.** This is not the same as *solving* problems. Some problems cannot be solved, but married couples need the ability to identify and analyze problems, propose and choose a possible solution, and follow it through. They will be able to solve *most* problems this way, and will learn to work around the ones they can't solve. The important thing is being committed to deal with problems, not walk away from them.

**4. Ability to give and receive love.** This is not as easy as it sounds, particularly for most men. Giving and receiving love comes more naturally for women. Men, on the other hand, have been taught in society that being manly or "macho" means not showing their sensitive side openly. As a result, many men have trouble expressing their true feelings. Marriage is a constant give-and-take, and this includes expression of love.

**5. Emotional stability.** This means being able to control our emotions and not let them run away from us. It means bridling our temper and not making excuses for immature emotional outbursts. Occasional loss of control is human but a pattern of it reveals a deeper problem. Anyone who constantly flies off the handle then says, "I can't help myself," is not being honest. If that is *truly* the case, then that person needs professional help. Usually, however, it is not a matter of being unable, but of being unwilling. Emotional stability means being willing and able to accept responsibility for our feelings, words, and actions.

**6. Ability to communicate.** True communication is not easy and happens rarely. Communication is the ability to ensure that people understand not only what you say but also what you mean. It is also the ability to listen to and understand others. Developing both of these aspects of communication takes a lot of time, patience, and hard work.

**7. Similarities between the couples themselves.** Any marriage involves the joining of two totally different people, but there should be some distinct similarities as well: common interests, common hobbies, a common faith, or similar political views for example. There needs to be some common meeting ground between the two.

**8. Similar family background.** Although this is not a highly critical factor—people of distinctly different backgrounds build successful marriages every day—similar family background is always helpful. A couple should enter marriage with all the advantages or "pluses" that they can, and similarity of family background is definitely a "plus."

\* \* \* \* \*

As important as they are, foundation stones alone are incomplete. They merely form the base upon which the completed structure must be built. The foundation stones of love, truth, trust, commitment, respect, submission, knowledge, faithfulness, patience, and financial stability are not ends in themselves. Rather they are bases upon which to build and display the beautiful jewel that we call marriage—a fusion of two distinct persons into one flesh, soul, and spirit. Success and happiness are no accident, but the result and reward of deliberate planning, diligent pursuit, and patient growth.

## PRINCIPLES

1.  Marriage is an investment, and success is directly proportional to the amount of knowledge and time invested in it.

2.  A successful marriage is the product of careful planning and deliberate design.

3.  Ten firm foundation stones for building a successful marriage:

    *   Love
    *   Truth
    *   Trust
    *   Commitment
    *   Respect
    *   Submission
    *   Knowledge
    *   Faithfulness
    *   Patience
    *   Financial stability

4.  Eight important "marriage ability" traits:

    *   Adaptability
    *   Empathy
    *   Ability to work through problems
    *   Ability to give and receive love
    *   Emotional stability

- Ability to communicate
- Similarities between the couples themselves
- Similar family background

CHAPTER SIX

# Loosing the Ties That Bind

$\mathcal{A}$ny experienced counselor will tell you that marital problems outnumber all other life and relationship problems combined. More problems arise in marriage than arise from drugs, crime, financial issues, or emotional or psychological disorders. It is a sobering sign of our times that an institution as critical to our culture and civilization as marriage should be in such crisis.

One of the toughest challenges newlywed couples face in adjusting to married life is learning how to relate to their parents and families of origin in light of their new circumstances. Marriage brings about fundamental changes in the relationships that exist between a couple and the families in which they grew up. Many newlyweds have trouble loosing the ties that bind them to their parents and to the lifestyle they knew as single adults. They often feel torn between their responsibility to their new spouse and their perceived responsibility to their parents. This tension creates conflict in the marriage, particularly when one partner finds it harder to let go than the other.

Adjustments to married life can be just as difficult for the parents of newlyweds as for the couple themselves. Sometimes parents compound the problem by trying to hold onto their married children, at least emotionally. Whether consciously or subconsciously, many parents try to make their children feel guilty for trying to break away on their own.

They struggle with the idea of their "baby" leaving the nest. If they have become emotionally or financially dependent on that child, they fear the changes that may come in that relationship because of the new person in their child's life.

Regardless of the direction from which it comes, confusion over how a newlywed couple should relate to their parents and families will cause stress in their marriage. Unless they learn how to deal with it, the "ties that bind" may become a noose that chokes the life out of their relationship.

## Marriage Is the Primary Human Relationship

According to the Bible, the highest and most important relationship of all is that between an individual human being and God. This is the fundamental and essential spiritual relationship. In the natural realm, and second only to the divine/human relationship, is the marriage relationship between a man and a woman. The husband/wife relationship is the primary human relationship. Problems always result when either of these relationships is removed from its position of priority. Most of the root causes of problems in life stem from people placing some other person or thing higher in their priority than either God or their spouse.

The relationship between husband and wife is primary because God established it first as the most basic human relationship.

> So the Lord God caused the man to fall into a deep sleep; and while he was sleeping, He took one of the man's ribs and closed up the place with flesh. Then the Lord God made a woman from the rib He had taken out of the man, and He brought her to the man. The man said, "This is now bone of my bones and flesh of my flesh; she shall be called 'woman,' for she was taken out of man." For this reason a man will leave his father and mother and be united to his wife, and they will become one flesh (Genesis 2:21-24).

*Notice that when God created the human race He began with a husband and wife, not a parent and child.* By God's design, the husband/wife relationship precedes and takes priority over the parent/child relationship. Verse 24 says that a man is to leave his father and mother and be united to his wife. The word "leave" suggests a temporary state while the word "united" indicates a permanent condition. In marriage a husband's and wife's primary responsibility is to each other, not to their parents or their siblings.

The husband and wife relationship is foundational and the key to every other relationship in life. Adam and Eve were husband and wife before they were parents. One reason the marriage relationship takes priority over the parent/child relationship is because a husband and wife make a covenant promise to meet each other's companionship needs for life. No such covenant exists between parents and their children. Parents have a responsibility to love and care for their children and to meet their physical, emotional, and spiritual needs, but this is fundamentally different from the "oneness" that they share as husband and wife.

 *The parent/child relationship is temporary and must be broken, while the husband/wife relationship is permanent and must not be broken.*

Essentially, the parent/child relationship is temporary and must be broken, while the husband/wife relationship is permanent and must not be broken. Parents should raise their children with the deliberate objective of seeing them grow into mature, *independent* adults. Once children are grown and on their own, a fundamental change occurs in their relationship with their parents. This change is even more pronounced once the children marry. Although parents should always be loved, honored, and respected, they no longer have the predominant place in the lives or priorities of their children. These married children have a new priority that takes precedence over their parents—their spouse. This is as it should be. The temporary relationship of parent/child gives way to the permanent relationship of husband/wife.

## Marriage Means Leaving Home

In some cultures it is customary to think of marriage as joining two families into one. The husband represents his family of origin, the wife represents hers, and together they and all their relatives become part of one big happy family. As common as this mentality may be in places, it is incorrect and unscriptural. *Marriage does not combine two families into one, but creates a third family.* When a husband and wife come together they form a distinct, separate, complete, and individual family unit that is independent of their respective families of origin. That is why Genesis 2:24 says, "For this reason a man will *leave his father and mother* and be united to his wife, and they will become one flesh" (emphasis added). In marriage, a man and a woman from two separate families join together to form a third family that is separate from the other two.

Although this verse speaks specifically of the husband leaving, it also includes the wife. How can a man be united to his wife unless she leaves home as well? It is only when they both leave their parents that they can successfully establish their own home. This verse emphasizes the man because he is the one who will become the head of the new family, the new decision-making unit established by this marriage.

One of the quickest roads to conflict in a marriage is when a husband has to compete with his wife's parents for priority of relationship. The same is true for a wife whose husband has trouble cutting the ties. This is why the instruction of the Scripture is so strong and so specific when it says that they are to *leave* their father and mother and be united to each other.

Leaving home is a fundamental principle of marriage. The first marriage-related instruction found in the Bible is the command to "leave." Although the main thought is that of leaving home, there is more to the idea than just physical departure. When a man and a woman marry they are to leave their families of origin not only physically, but also mentally, financially, and emotionally. This does not mean they must sever all future connections with their families, but it does mean that their families should not play a significant role in the decisions they make as a couple or in the way they build their home and marriage. Leaving means that a married couple is neither burdened by nor a burden to their parents.

 *When a man and a woman marry they are to leave their families of origin not only physically, but also mentally, financially, and emotionally.*

The word *leave* implies that the family of origin may or may not want them to go. Many parents struggle with this very thing, finding it hard to let go of their children and allow them to live their own lives as mature and independent adults. That is why God in His wisdom does not leave the option to the parents. When an adult child gets married and leaves the nest, he or she is saying, "I'm ready to live my own life now. I have chosen this person to spend the rest of my life with. I love you, but I have to make my own decisions. No matter how you feel, I'm leaving. Your opinion matters to me, but I can't let it be the determining factor in what I do. I have to choose what is right for me."

Many young people would rather not leave home until they get their parents' consent. While this is not a scriptural requirement, there is certainly nothing wrong with it. Leaving home with your parents' blessing is always nice, but it is also okay to leave home without it. The primary consideration is doing God's will. It is more important to obey God than to obey your parents' wishes. Staying home to satisfy their desires after God has told you to leave is to disobey God.

## Cultivating Companionship

There are many reasons why it is essential for young married couples to leave home physically and emotionally. One of the most important is to give them the opportunity from the very beginning of their marriage to cultivate companionship with each other. Companionship is the basis for all successful marriage. The parent/child relationship is established by birth or adoption, but the husband/wife relationship is established by covenant, and there is a difference. Because marriage is a covenant established by God and sealed by the Holy Spirit, it supercedes blood ties. Blood may be thicker than water, but it is not thicker than promise.

 *The parent/child relationship is established by birth or adoption, but the husband/wife relationship is established by covenant.*

In marriage, our spouse is more important than any other person on earth. Other than the Lord, no one, and I mean *no one*, should take precedence over our husband or our wife either in our attention or our affection. We should give deference to each other ahead of parents, siblings, or any other ties of blood or family. The opinions, desires, or demands of family members no longer hold sway. Spouses must give each other first place. They need to take time to be alone together, to get to know each other not only as spouses and lovers but also as friends and lifelong companions. Companionship in marriage is more important than circumstances of blood or birth.

 *Companionship in marriage is more important than circumstances of blood or birth.*

Like any other worthwhile endeavor, building companionship requires patience, time, and hard work. Companionship must be cultivated. Anyone who desires to have a beautiful garden must be willing to take the time to turn and prepare the soil, add fertilizer, plant the seeds, irrigate carefully, pull up weeds diligently, and give patient, daily attention to the new plants. Companionship in marriage must be nurtured with the same degree of care. It will not develop overnight or accidentally. Any "weeds" that would choke out the developing flower of companionship must be rooted out.

One of those "weeds" that troubles far too many marriages is the well-intentioned but inappropriate interference of family members into the daily affairs of the couple's life and relationship. Once a man and woman have married, the only thing they should receive from their parents is advice and counsel, and then *only* when they ask for it. Parents should not offer opinions or advice without being asked. To do so undermines the development of the leadership and self-determination of the couple. When they married, the leadership and decision-making responsibilities transferred from their former homes to the new home they are building together. All leadership now devolves on them. They are responsible for making their own decisions. Part of cultivating companionship is learning how to exercise these responsibilities effectively together.

How critical is this principle of independence for the success of a new marriage? It is so vital that the couple, even at the risk of sounding rude or hurting feelings, must do whatever is necessary to prevent their parents or other family members from imposing their opinions or advice uninvited. It may not be easy, but it is necessary in order to be obedient to God's Word.

## Should Children Support Their Parents?

Many young couples just starting out in married life struggle with understanding what responsibilities they now have toward their parents. A common attitude in the Bahamas, where I live, is for parents to expect their grown children, even those who are married, to support them financially and in other ways on an ongoing basis. After all, it is only right for children to "repay" their parents in this way for raising and taking care of them. This attitude is not unique to the Bahamas, or even to the third world. To a greater or lesser degree it is found in every culture, particularly in families and ethnic groups where traditional generational ties are very strong.

Is this attitude correct? Are married children responsible for supporting their parents? To find the answer we need to look to the Bible, the Word of the God who originally designed marriage and the family. Consider what Paul, the first-century Christian missionary, theologian, and writer had to say:

> *Now I am ready to visit you for the third time, and I will not be a burden to you, because what I want is not your possessions but you. After all, children should not have to save up for their parents, but parents for their children* (2 Corinthians 12:14).

 *True independence works both ways: Children are not dependent on their parents, and parents are not dependent on their children.*

Although in context Paul was referring to the believers in the church in Corinth as his spiritual "children," the principle applies also in the realm of human family relations: "Children should not have to save up for their parents, but parents for their children." Paul pledged to the Corinthian church that he would not be a burden to them when he visited. In the same manner, parents should not be a burden to their children, either financially or in any other way. On the contrary, this verse says that parents should "save up" for their children. Parents have the responsibility to support their children and do everything they can to prepare the way for their children to become mature, productive, and independent adults. True independence works both ways: Children are not dependent on their parents, and parents are not dependent on their children.

Adjusting to married life is challenging enough without the couple feeling the pressure of guilt or custom to support their parents. They need the freedom to establish their own home, set up their own budget, and determine their own priorities. This does not mean that they should have no concern for their parents' welfare. If their parents are truly in need, and if the couple genuinely has the means to help, fine. The decision to help should be a choice freely made by the couple together, however, and not imposed on them from outside as a custom or expectation.

At the same time, the Bible clearly indicates that children do bear some responsibility for the welfare of their parents, particularly those who are widowed or who have no legitimate means of caring for themselves. Jesus Himself, even while hanging on the cross, made a point as the eldest son of His earthly family to commit His mother into the care of John, His disciple and close friend (see Jn. 19:26-27). James speaks of believers' responsibility to "look after orphans and widows in their distress" (Jas. 1:27b). Orphans and widows represented the lowest and most powerless classes of society in that day—people who had no one to speak for them. Although James' instructions are to the Church as a whole, undoubtedly some of these orphans and widows had children or other relatives in the Church.

In the fifth chapter of First Timothy, Paul provides practical counsel for dealing with a specific situation involving widows.

> *Give proper recognition to those widows who are really in need. But if a widow has children or grandchildren, these should learn first of all to put their religion into practice by caring for their own family and so repaying their parents and grandparents, for this is pleasing to God....If anyone does*

*not provide for his relatives, and especially for his immediate*
*family, he has denied the faith and is worse than an unbe-*
*liever* (1 Timothy 5:3-4,8).

The church in this case had a responsibility and ministry to care for widows who were "really in need." These were women who without their husbands had no one else to care for them. Many of these men may have died as martyrs for their faith. Persecution could have so greatly swollen the ranks of widows who needed help that the resources of the church were severely taxed. Paul said that the Church's primary responsibility was to those widows who had no one— not even children or grandchildren—to take care of them. Widows who had children or grandchildren in the Church were the responsibility of those children or grandchildren.

In other words, children or grandchildren are responsible under God for caring for parents or grandparents who, because of health, destitution, or other reasons, *cannot care for themselves*. Parents who are healthy and possess the means of supporting themselves should not become burdens to their children. Children, on the other hand, have the responsibility to provide for the welfare of parents who can no longer provide for themselves.

## Establish Relationship Parameters up Front

Much conflict and confusion between a married couple and their respective families could be avoided by simply taking the time at the beginning to establish clear parameters for how these families will relate to each other, and making sure that everyone involved understands those parameters. This is one important purpose of the engagement period. Engagement is not only to provide time for the couple to get to know each other and to plan their wedding, but to allow members of the two families involved to get acquainted as well.

*A married couple should take time at the beginning of their marriage to establish clear parameters for how their families will relate to each other, and make sure that everyone involved understands those parameters.*

During the engagement the couple should thoroughly discuss their philosophies of life and agree on the principles that will guide their marriage. They should share their dreams, identify their goals, and plan their strategy for realizing those dreams and goals. They should come to a mutual understanding regarding financial planning, including investments, savings, and an ongoing household budget. Everything the couple does during this planning period should be for the purpose of establishing safeguards to protect both them and their marriage.

It is important for the members of both families to understand that this marriage will create a new, separate family, resulting in certain fundamental changes in the way the couple relates to them. Let's consider a couple of common scenarios that can cause great problems for everyone if not handled correctly.

Suppose that prior to getting married a young man (let's call him John) has had a good job and has helped his parents out with their bills and other expenses. There is nothing particularly unusual about this arrangement, particularly if he was living at home. If his parents have come to rely on his financial assistance, his upcoming marriage may create a crisis for them. What will they do? How will they make it if their son no longer helps out?

One day not long after the wedding John receives a phone call from his mother. "John," she says, "you've always been so good to help out when we needed it. Our light bill is coming due and we're a little short of money. Can you help out?" At this point John has three choices. He can say no, he can say yes, or he can say, "Let me talk it over with Sarah" (his wife). "We'll have to see if it will fit in with our budget."

If John values his relationship with his mother, he probably will not give her a flat "no." If he values peace and harmony in his marriage he will not give her an immediate "yes." If he is smart, he will discuss her request with Sarah before making a final decision. Since John and Sarah worked out their financial plan together and established their budget together, they need to decide together on any changes to their plan. Their first priority is the strength and stability of their own home and circumstances. If their budget allows them to assist with his mother's light bill, and they both agree to it, fine. Then, the help is coming from both of them, and not just from "mama's little boy." If not, then they need to tell her gently but clearly, "I'm sorry, but we cannot help this time."

When John and Sarah married, they became each other's number one priority. If they have established this understanding up front with each other and with their parents, they will avoid a lot of heartache and hurt feelings.

Another common problem newlyweds sometimes face is when parents or other family just "drop in" uninvited and make themselves at home, or offer unsolicited opinions or advice. There are times when married couples simply want to be alone together, and during such times nothing cranks up the tension level as much as the unexpected arrival of family.

Suppose John's mother and sister drop in uninvited. Sister goes immediately to the refrigerator and helps herself to some leftovers. John's mother looks at the new rug on the floor and says, "I don't like that rug. I think you ought to get another one." At this point, John is in a dilemma. He doesn't want to hurt his mother or his sister, yet Sarah is standing quietly at one side of the room fuming. John's sister has invaded her house unannounced and raided her refrigerator uninvited.

What's even worse, John's mother has just criticized the new rug that Sarah picked out herself, thereby criticizing Sarah and her sense of taste. A potential explosion is brewing.

The situation may not blow up while John's mother and sister are there, but it will after they leave. If Sarah complains, John may become defensive and make matters worse. After all, this is *his* family she is criticizing. Unless John deals with the problem, Sarah's resentment may grow until the next time she sees his mother and sister, when she "tells them off." This is guaranteed to poison Sarah's relationship with John's family.

In this kind of disagreement the worst thing to do is to let the opposite partner confront the family. The right thing is for *John* to go to his mother and sister and say, "I don't appreciate your coming over unannounced. Mom, your comment about the rug was uncalled for and it hurt Sarah's feelings. Sis, you have no right to just help yourself to our food when you come over." They may get angry and pout for awhile, but at least John is *family*, and by confronting the issue with them himself he has protected Sarah and removed her as the focus of their anger and resentment.

These are only two examples of common problems involving a married couple's relationship to their families, but the principle should be clear.

A husband's top priority is to protect his wife and a wife's, her husband. Together they are committed to protecting each other, preserving their marriage, and cultivating their companionship. Loosing the ties that bind a husband and wife to their families is not always easy but it is necessary. Establishing parameters in advance for the loosening of those ties will make the process easier for everyone and give a new marriage one of those "pluses" that is so important for success.

## PRINCIPLES

1. The husband/wife relationship is the primary human relationship.

2. The husband and wife relationship is foundational and the key to every other relationship in life.

3. Leaving home is a fundamental principle of marriage.

4. Companionship is the basis for all successful marriage.

5. Companionship in marriage is more important than circumstances of blood or birth.

6. Parents who are healthy and possess the means of supporting themselves should not become burdens to their children. Children, on the other hand, have the responsibility to provide for the welfare of parents who can no longer provide for themselves.

7. At the beginning of a marriage, the couple should establish clear parameters for how their families will relate to each other.

8. A husband's top priority is to protect his wife and a wife's, her husband. Together they are committed to protecting each other, preserving their marriage, and cultivating their companionship.

## CHAPTER SEVEN

# *Vive la Difference!*

$L$et's face it, men and women are different. There is no doubt about it. Although the obvious physical differences have been noted and appreciated from the very beginning, it is only in the last generation or so that the essential psychological and emotional differences between men and women have been identified and confirmed scientifically.

The male and female of the human species are "wired" differently. They do not think, speak, or act the same way in response to the same stimuli. Men and women send, receive, and process information differently. Because they view the world through different mental and emotional "filters," men and women can look at the same thing and see completely different aspects. They can be exposed to the same information and draw totally dissimilar conclusions. They can examine the same data and yet be poles apart in how they interpret that data.

Needless to say, this fundamental difference in the way men and women think and act lies at the heart of much of the conflict, confusion, and misunderstanding that has occurred between the sexes for centuries. Communication problems between men and women are so commonplace as to be proverbial. Does this sound familiar? "I just don't understand him (or her). Whenever we try to talk, it's as though we are on different wavelengths." Have you ever heard anyone say, "Isn't that just like a woman!" or "He's acting just like a man!"

As with anything else, knowledge can banish confusion where male/female relations are concerned. Understanding not only that men and women *are* different but also *how* they are different is vital to improving male/female communication and relationships at every level. This knowledge is particularly critical for young couples who want to ensure that their marriage has the greatest chances of success and happiness.

In the beginning, God created man as a spirit and placed that spirit in two flesh and blood "houses"—male and female. This "joining" of the male and female "houses" is the *only* God-ordained method for producing *new* "houses." The basic purpose of male and female "houses" is to produce new houses.

A spirit has no gender. Whether man or woman, all members of the human race have the same spirit, the same essence. Males and females, however, have biological and psychological differences according to God's design. He made the male house different from the female house because they have different functions.

 *The male is "wired" for logic. The female, on the other hand, is "wired" for emotional response.*

Males and females have different chemical and hormonal balances which cause them to think and behave differently. Because God intended for the male to be the head of the family unit, He endowed him chemically and hormonally for logical thinking. The male is "wired" for logic. The female, on the other hand, is "wired" for emotional response. Her body's chemical and hormonal balance sets her up to operate from a feelings-based center. Because both genders have both male and female hormones, "logical" males have an "emotional" side and "emotional" females have a "logical" side. In general, however, males and females view the world according to how they are wired—males from a logical center and females from an emotional center.

## Fifteen Essential Differences Between Men and Women

Many husbands and wives suffer needlessly from confusion, misunderstanding, and hurt feelings simply because they do not understand each other's fundamental differences. Let's consider fifteen specific ways that men and women differ, all of which can have a profound effect on how they relate to each other, particularly in the context of marriage. These fifteen statements are not intended to lump all men and women indiscriminately into one group or the other—there are always exceptions to every rule—but they are *generally* true of most men and women with regard to their psychological and emotional makeup.

**1. A man is a logical thinker while a woman is an emotional feeler.**

To be logical means to think in a reasoned, organized, and orderly manner. A logical thinker has an analytical mind that works like a computer, processing and evaluating information in a precise and predictable pattern. If one plus one equals two, then two cut in half is two ones; that's logic. In general, that's the way men think. They look for the facts and act accordingly.

Women are emotional. They approach issues more from feelings than from reason. This is not a bad thing. Being emotionally centered is neither better nor worse than being logical; it is just different. Another way of looking at it is to say that a man leads with his mind while a woman leads with her heart.

While logic and emotion might seem incompatible on the surface, in reality they complement each other very well. What kind of world would this be if everyone was exclusively logical? Life would be rather empty, with no spirit, no passion, no fire, and little or no art. At the same time, emotion without logic would result in life without order. Both logic and emotion are necessary, not only for fulfillment but for survival. This reveals the brilliance of God's design.

 *A man leads with his mind while a woman leads with her heart.*

Here's an example. John and Sarah are standing in their living room and John notices that an armchair is blocking easy access to the air conditioner. He says, "That chair is in the way. We need to move it." He is thinking logically. At the same time, Sarah is thinking how nicely the chair offsets the couch and the curtains and how beautiful a vase of flowers would look on the end table next to it. She is thinking emotionally. Neither viewpoint is right or wrong, or better or worse than the other one. They are just different. If John and Sarah understand that they view the same situation in two different ways, they can reach a common consensus.

In general, men are logical and women are emotional.

**2. For a woman, language spoken is an expression of what she is feeling. For a man, language spoken is an expression of what he is thinking.**

A woman says what is on her heart while a man says what is on his mind. This is another expression of the emotion/logic dichotomy between the ways women and men think. Women are emotional feelers and their spoken words need to be understood from that frame of reference. Men are logical, and their words often do not adequately express their true feelings. Both may have similar thoughts or feelings but will express them in different ways. Unless they understand this difference, a married couple will experience communication problems.

 *A woman says what is on her heart while a man says what is on his mind.*

Let's suppose that John has promised to pick up Sarah at 5:00, right after work. John is running late and the later he gets the more steamed Sarah becomes. She is pacing and sweating and fuming and rehearsing in her mind the speech she will give John when she sees him.

John finally pulls up at 6:00. Giving Sarah a sheepish grin he says, "Hi. I'm sorry I'm late." John really means it; he *is* sorry he's late. He's telling Sarah what he's thinking. He may have trouble showing how sorry he is, but at least he thought enough to apologize. Ignoring John's words, Sarah slides into the passenger seat, slams the door and sits right up next to it, as far away from John as possible. She says nothing as John drives off.

After several minutes of complete silence, John asks, "What's wrong?" As far as he is concerned the matter is finished. He was late, he apologized, end of story. Everybody has a right to be late once in awhile. That's his logical thinking at work.

"Nothing's wrong," Sarah snaps.

After several more minutes of silence, John tries again. "Why don't we go out for dinner? I'll take you to a really nice place."

"No. I don't want to go out."

Pulling up to a florist, John makes another attempt. "I just want to run in here and get some flowers."

"For who? If you loved me that much you'd have been there at 5:00 like you said you would."

Through all of this, John should not listen to what Sarah is saying as much as listen to how she is feeling. Sometimes when a person tries to tell how he or she feels, the words don't come out right. Logical John needs to understand emotional Sarah. At the same time, Sarah needs to realize that John has already said what was on his mind. They both have a responsibility to understand what lies beyond spoken words and minister to each other.

**3. Language that is heard by a woman is an emotional experience. Language that is heard by a man is the receiving of information.**

When a woman speaks, although she may be expressing what she feels, a man will usually hear it as information, often on an impersonal level. When a man speaks, even if he is simply saying what's on his mind, a woman will usually receive his words at a much deeper personal and emotional level.

It is easy to see how conflict could develop because of this. John offers to take Sarah out for dinner, but she says, "No. I don't want to go out." John hears that as information: "Okay, she doesn't want to go out." The problem is that Sarah is saying what she is feeling, not what she is thinking. Sarah is thinking, "I'm so mad at you. You kept me waiting for an hour and now you have the nerve to suggest we go to dinner as though nothing happened? Not so fast, mister."

 *Hearing is not the same as understanding. What one person says may not be what the other person hears.*

Because John receives spoken language as information, he has completely missed the deeper level of where Sarah is emotionally. She, on the other hand, interprets his words as shallow, uncaring, and inadequate. Both are sincerely trying to communicate but are not connecting because they do not understand each other's frame of reference.

Hearing is not the same as understanding. What one person says may not be what the other person hears. That is why communication is such an art. Husbands need to remember that every word they say will be received by their wives as an emotional experience. Wives need to keep in mind that every word they say will be received by their husbands as information. In order to understand each other better, husbands and wives both should learn to think in terms of how the other receives and interprets their words, and speak accordingly.

**4. Women tend to take everything personally. Men tend to take everything impersonally.**

This difference is directly related to the way men and women are "wired": Men are logical thinkers and women are emotional feelers. A woman interprets everything from an emotional perspective while a man is looking for information. John may remark to Sarah, "Honey, I don't like the way your hair looks today." He is imparting information and even though he includes the qualifier "today," Sarah doesn't hear that. All she hears is "I don't like the way your hair looks." What John offered as information Sarah interprets emotionally, and becomes angry and hurt. As a result, she may rush off to the hairdresser and get a new cut or a new style, and all the while John is wondering why she is making such a big deal of the whole thing. It is because she took it personally.

Sarah may say to John, "Those pants don't look good on you. They are not hanging right." John's response may be, "Okay, no big deal. I'll change it tomorrow when I change clothes." He has received her criticism as information, and has filed it away in his mind like a computer. He may take action in response to her comment but he doesn't take it personally.

Because women tend to take everything personally, men need to learn to be careful what they say to women and how they say it. A woman will remember an irritating action or an offhand comment for years. On the other hand, because men take things impersonally, women must be careful in how they interpret men's responses to what they say. Just because a man does not react emotionally in the same way as a woman does not mean that he has no feelings or that he does not care. He is looking for information and trying to determine an appropriate way to respond.

**5. Women are interested in the details—the "nitty-gritty." Men are interested in the principle—the abstract or the philosophy.**

Sarah asks John, "How was your day?" and he answers, "Fine." That's not the kind of answer Sarah was looking for. She wants to hear the step-by-step, moment-by-moment details of John's day. She isn't trying to pry; that's just the way she thinks. John's simple response reflects the way he thinks: "I had a good day, it was great. Now, let's move on to something else." He is focusing on the principle (he had a good day) not on the nitty-gritty details (I did this and that and thus and so).

Suppose John invites another couple to come over for dinner. He is focusing on the principle that he wants to be hospitable to his friends. As soon as he tells Sarah, she immediately looks at all the details. What will we fix for dinner? What dishes should we use? How should we set the table? What about that ragged carpet in the living room? The drapes are dirty; can we get them cleaned? What about that spot on the wall?

All John is thinking about is hosting their friends for a fun evening. He isn't worrying about the drapes or the dirty wall or the ragged carpet or the dishes. A simple principle for him may be an ordeal of details for Sarah.

Leaders need to think in principles and concepts, not the nitty-gritty details. Managers and company presidents don't have time to focus on the details. Their responsibility is to consider the principles, the philosophy of where the company is going, and to determine goals. A leader sets the vision and direction, and those under the leader work out the details to accomplish the vision. Under God's design for the home, the husband sets the vision and direction—the principles. That is his gift and role. The wife is gifted to know how to bring the vision to fruition—the details. Together it is a powerful combination.

**6. In material things, women tend to look at goals only. Men want to know the details of how to get there.**

Sarah dreams of all the different things she would like to have for herself and her family: some new jewelry, a new refrigerator, a new car, a new house. While John may have the same dreams and desires, he may not voice them as plainly because, in his logical and analytical way of thinking, he focuses on the practical aspects and challenges of those dreams. How are we going to do this? Where are we going to get the money? Will our budget allow for a new refrigerator right now? Do we have the means to buy a new car?

It's easy to see how this could create conflict and misunderstanding in a marriage. Sarah gets upset and angry because John does not seem to share her dream with the same level of enthusiasm as she. In her opinion he is dragging his feet as if he does not really care whether or not they realize their dreams. At the same time, John is frustrated with Sarah because she does not seem to understand the financial realities. "What is it with this woman? Does she think money grows on trees?" It's not that John doesn't share what Sarah's dreams; he is concerned with the practical nuts-and-bolts details of how to make those dreams come true.

*In material things, women focus on the what and men focus on the how.*

In material things women are concerned with goals and men are concerned with getting there. To state it another way, women focus on the what and men focus on the how.

**7. In spiritual or intangible things, men look at goals. Women want to know how to get there.**

In the spiritual realm, men focus on the goal while women want to know the details. Once again, this difference between men and women is part of God's design. Spiritually, the husband is supposed to be the head of the home, and therefore needs to know the direction, the goals, and the objectives for the spiritual growth and development of the family. The wife is interested in the details, the specifics of how they are going to reach their spiritual goals. This is the exact opposite of the material realm. In this case, men focus on the what and women focus on the how.

John tells Sarah that their goal as a family is to grow close to the Lord. That is the vision, the principle. When Sarah asks "How?" John proposes, "Let's have prayer with each other and with the children every morning before work, and an hour of Bible study together every evening." That is a good plan and bears fruit as long as they follow it. If John reaches a point where he does not follow through, Sarah will become frustrated.

 *In spiritual things, men focus on the what and women focus on the how.*

Failure of men to take and maintain the spiritual lead in their homes and marriages is one of the biggest problems in the family today. Countless wives have been forced by default to assume the spiritual leadership in their homes because their husbands either will not or cannot carry out that role. This is not as it should be. Wives can be of great value in helping plan the specifics for reaching marriage and family spiritual goals, but the husband should be the visionary, the one who determines the direction and sets the pace.

**8. A man's mind is like a filing cabinet. A woman's mind is like a computer.**

Show a man a problem or a task that needs to be done and he will take the information, file it away in his mind, close the drawer, and deal with it when he can. In the meantime, he continues with other things. A woman will identify a problem or a task and, like a computer that is running all the time, not relax until the problem is dealt with or the task completed.

Sarah comes to John and says, "The bathroom walls need to be painted." John answers, "Okay," and files the information away. He doesn't forget about it, but is waiting until a better or more appropriate time to do it. As far as John is concerned, the matter is at rest. Sarah identified the task, passed it on to John, and he has processed the information. He *will* do it.

Two days go by. Sarah says, "The bathroom walls still haven't been painted." Her mind will not rest on this subject until the job is done. John, however, is a little annoyed by her reminder. "I know. I haven't forgotten. I'll do it. Just give me some time." A wife should be sensitive to her husband's "filing cabinet" approach to thinking, and give him room to do the things he has said he will do. A husband, on the other hand, should be sensitive to the way his wife's mind works, and try to respond in as timely a manner as possible. This involves a fair amount of give-and-take on both sides.

**9. A woman's home is an extension of her personality. A man's job is an extension of his personality.**

It's easy for a woman to get wrapped up in her home and her husband not understand why, and for a man to get caught up in his work and his wife be just as puzzled. A woman can work for years and never become attached to her job. It is different with a man. His job becomes a part of him, a part of his self-identity. A man's career is an extension of his personality. A woman can detach herself from her job and immerse herself in her home. A man will often bring his job home with him, at least in his mind and attitude, if not physically. John's job is to him a symbol of his manhood, his self-worth, and his ability to provide for Sarah and their children. Sarah should be sensitive to this and careful never to berate or belittle John with regard to his work. If she criticizes his job or career choice, she is criticizing him.

In the same way, a woman's home is an extension of her personality. Anything that touches a woman's home touches her, because her home represents who she is and how she sees herself. That's why a woman normally is very sensitive about the condition and appearance of her home. Quite often, husbands do not adequately understand this. They do not fully appreciate how important the physical aspects of their residence are to their wives' sense of pride and self-esteem. When a woman talks about her house, she is talking about herself. If Sarah tells John they need new living room curtains, he needs to be sensitive to what she is really saying. The curtains may look fine to him, but Sarah may see things that he misses. For her sake John needs to learn to see their house through her eyes and not just his own.

**10. Men can be nomadic. Women need security and roots.**

A woman needs to be constantly reassured that she is grounded and secure in her marriage relationship. She needs to be continually affirmed that she is the most important person in her husband's life. He needs to tell her regularly and often that he loves her. It's not enough for him to assume that she knows this; she needs to hear it. It's not that she does not believe or trust her husband, it's just the way she is made. A man does not need the same kind of emotional stroking as a woman.

 *Constant reassurance brings security.*

A man is like a camel, in that he can take one "drink" and go for a long time. A woman is like the deer of Psalm 42:1 that "pants for streams of water." She needs a "drink" more often. Because of their nomadic nature, men usually find it easier to be by themselves than women do. Wives often have trouble understanding that there are times when their husbands simply want to be alone for awhile. If a wife is in the least bit insecure in her relationship with her husband, she may read this as rejection or as a sign that she no longer satisfies him. That's why he needs to be sensitive and careful to reassure her of his love through both his words and his actions. Constant reassurance brings security.

Most men can pull up stakes and move around easily, but women need roots. They want to be settled. It's easy for a guy to just pick up and change, but it's not as easy for a woman, because she is an emotional feeler and becomes more attached to places and things than a man does. With this in mind, a husband needs to be aware that he cannot simply get up and move without considering his wife's need for the security of "settled-ness."

**11. Women tend to be guilt prone. Men tend to be resentful.**

Because of her emotion-centered base a woman is prone to blame herself and take responsibility for anything that goes wrong in a relationship, even if it is not really her fault. Sometimes she will even rehearse over and over in her head a list of reasons why she is to blame. Many women walk around every day under a cloud of guilt that quite often they have placed there themselves and which is usually unjustified. When problems arise in their relationships women tend to second-guess themselves. "What did I say to make him mad? What could I have done to keep us from fighting?" Many times it is not the woman's fault at all, but she still has trouble accepting that.

A man is different. When something goes wrong in a relationship he will resent the woman or even another man before he will acknowledge his own responsibility. Many men will do almost anything to avoid carrying around a sense of personal guilt. They would rather lash out in anger than accept blame.

These two responses are opposites and feed off of each other. A man will refuse to accept his guilt while a woman will take upon herself even guilt that is not her own. She then becomes an object of the man's resentment and anger, an easy target for his spite as he acts out against the guilt that he refuses to bear. Married couples need to be very watchful and wary of these tendencies because they can destroy a relationship more quickly than almost anything else.

**12. Men are stable and level off. Women are always changing.**

Once again, this difference between men and women is due to the specific chemical and hormonal balances in their bodies and the particular frame of reference—logical or emotional—from which they operate. Many men would say that few things aggravate them as much as a woman who is always changing her mind. Women, on the other hand, would argue that men often seem to be unfazed—even cold or callous—no matter what happens. This is primarily a difference in perspective.

In general, a man can make a decision and stick with it, even to the point of stubbornness. A woman may tell him one thing and then a few minutes later say, "I've changed my mind." Neither trait is better or worse than the other; they merely reveal the different ways that men's and women's mental processes work.

Suppose that John and Sarah are preparing to go to a banquet. John chooses his gray suit and puts it on. Now he waits as Sarah tries first her blue dress, then her red dress, then her lavender dress...and finally settles on the blue dress she tried on first. Like her home, Sarah's clothes make a personal statement. Everything has to be perfect; she has to look just right. All the while John is fidgeting and thinking, *Choose something, for Pete's sake, and let's go!* As long as his suit is clean and his tie is straight he's fine.

*Stability and spontaneity—both are important for a healthy and fulfilling relationship.*

Another way to look at this difference is to say that men are more stable or stolid while women are more spontaneous. Stability and spontaneity—both are important for a healthy and fulfilling relationship. Stability provides necessary grounding while spontaneity injects a healthy dose of adventure.

**13. Women tend to become involved more easily and more quickly than men do. Men tend to stand back and evaluate before they get involved.**

Because they are emotionally centered, women are more apt than men to involve themselves quickly in a cause or movement or project. Women tend to lead with their hearts. They see a need or recognize a noble or worthy cause that touches their hearts, and off they go. Logic-driven men, however, lead with their minds, and tend to hold themselves aloof and apart, carefully observing and evaluating before they commit themselves. Because of their logical focus men tend to be skeptical and must analyze something from every direction before joining themselves to it. Although it may take a man longer to come around, once he makes a decision he is every bit as committed as a woman. Men and women may travel by different roads but eventually they arrive at the same destination.

 *Reason and emotion complement each other.*

Here again the genius of God's design is revealed. Reason and emotion complement each other. Together they bring completeness to life and faith. Logic without passion is dry, austere, and lifeless. Passion without logic lacks order and stability. Married couples who understand and appreciate the inter-connectedness of logic and emotion have a much higher probability of building a stable marriage characterized by strength, love, and a passionate zest for life.

**14. Men need to be told again and again. Women never forget.**

A man's mind is like a filing cabinet; anything spoken to him he files away for later retrieval. Just because he doesn't act on it immediately does not mean he has forgotten or ignored what he was told. He has simply filed it away. That's why it so often seems as though a man needs to be told or reminded again and again. A woman's mind is like a computer that never forgets anything, but keeps it ready for immediate recall on demand. Women never forget anything they say to a man or anything that a man says to them, and they also make sure that he doesn't forget.

Either of these qualities may be negative or positive depending on the situation. Because they tend to receive things impersonally, men are more apt to overlook or forget disparaging comments made by them or to them. Generally, men are less prone to hold a grudge. However, on the negative side, this "forgetfulness" can cause men to become terribly insensitive and unresponsive to the needs of their wives and children.

Because a woman receives everything emotionally and holds words and feelings close to her heart, she is naturally more sensitive and responsive to the needs she sees around her. On the down side, a woman's tendency to remember everything and take everything personally can cause her to allow a hurt or an insult or an offense to fester and grow for weeks, months, and even years, creating continual stress, anger, and heartache.

How can husbands and wives deal with these differences effectively in their relationships? Husbands must be careful what they say and how they say it, remembering the wise counsel of the Book of Proverbs: "A gentle answer turns away wrath, but a harsh word stirs up anger" (Prov. 15:1). Wives should temper their remembering with grace, in accordance with the words of Paul: "[Love] is not easily angered, it keeps no record of wrongs" (1 Cor. 13:5b).

**15. Men tend to remember the gist of things rather than the details. Women tend to remember the details and sometimes distort the gist.**

This is akin to the old "he said, she said" controversy. Men tend to remember conversations or events in general overview, while women recall specific details with laser-like precision. Women sometimes accuse men of hedging on what they said they would do when in reality the men simply cannot recall the specifics of the conversation. Men are clear on the gist of what was said, but the details are less important. Women are sharp on the details but sometimes not as clear in remembering the gist.

Both tendencies can distort the truth. Recalling the gist without the details is like trying to describe an elephant seen dimly in a fog: "All I know is, it was big." Fixating on the details is like four blindfolded people in a room trying to describe that same elephant from touch alone. One touches the leg, another the trunk, the third the tail, and the fourth an ear. Their descriptions will be quite different from each other.

This difference in the manner of recall between men and women is one of the most basic causes for communication problems between them. Sarah reminds John of a previous conversation and he admits, "Yes, I think I did say something like that."

"No," Sarah replies, "that is *exactly* what you said."

"Well, that's not what I meant."

"Maybe not, but that's what you said."

John remembers the gist of the conversation and Sarah remembers the specifics. This kind of communication confusion is summed up pretty well in the statement: "I know you think you understand what you thought I said, but I'm not sure you realize that what you heard is not what I meant."

As always, patience and understanding go a long way in relieving the tension and stress created by the natural differences that distinguish men and women and the way they think.

* * * *

A common complaint in male/female relationship problems is "You just don't understand me" or, in other words, "You want me to be just like you." That is simply not the way things are, and we should not wish it otherwise. Men and women are different, and thank God that they are.

A husband should not expect or desire his wife to start thinking in the logical and analytically centered way he does. Likewise, a wife should not look to her husband to see things through her emotional framework. Both should learn to value and celebrate the vital differences that God has built into each gender of the creature called *man*.

Look how those differences complement each other. A world of logic without feelings would be a world populated by mindless and heartless computers. God did not create computers. He created man—male and female—and endowed them with all the varied and complementary qualities that are necessary for rich and full living.

Men and women are not the same, and for good reason. Celebrate the difference!

# PRINCIPLES

1. A man is a logical thinker while a woman is an emotional feeler.

2. For a woman, language spoken is an expression of what she is feeling. For a man, language spoken is an expression of what he is thinking.

3. Language that is heard by a woman is an emotional experience. Language that is heard by a man is the receiving of information.

4. Women tend to take everything personally. Men tend to take everything impersonally.

5. Women are interested in the details—the "nitty-gritty." Men are interested in the principle—the abstract or the philosophy.

6. In material things, women tend to look at goals only. Men want to know the details of how to get there.

7. In spiritual or intangible things, men look at goals. Women want to know how to get there.

8. A man's mind is like a filing cabinet. A woman's mind is like a computer.

9. A woman's home is an extension of her personality. A man's job is an extension of his personality.

10. Men can be nomadic. Women need security and roots.

11. Women tend to be guilt prone. Men tend to be resentful.

12. Men are stable and level off. Women are always changing.

13. Women tend to become involved more easily and more quickly than men do. Men tend to stand back and evaluate before they get involved.

14. Men need to be told again and again. Women never forget.

15. Men tend to remember the gist of things rather than the details. Women tend to remember the details and sometimes distort the gist.

### ✑ CHAPTER EIGHT ✑

# *Friendship: The Highest Relationship of All*

$\mathcal{T}$he husband/wife relationship is the oldest and most preeminent of all human relationships. It predates and goes ahead of any other relationship, including parent/child, mother/daughter, father/son, and sister/brother. No relationship should be closer, more personal, or more intimate than that which exists between a husband and wife. Such intimacy involves not only love but also knowledge. A husband and wife should know each other better than they know anyone else in the world. They should know each other's likes and dislikes, their quirks and pet peeves, their strengths and weaknesses, their good and bad qualities, their gifts and talents, their prejudices and blind spots, their graces and their character flaws. In short, a husband and wife should know everything about each other, even those undesirable traits that they hide from everyone else.

 *Relationship does not guarantee knowledge.*

This kind of knowledge is not automatic. It does not happen simply because two people get married. Relationship does not guarantee knowledge. One of the greatest problems in marriage or any other human relationship involves the labels we use.

Words like "husband" and "wife," "mother" and "daughter," "sister" and "brother," or "father" and "son" describe various relational connections within a family. They also imply a knowledge or intimacy that may or may not exist.

For example, a mother and daughter may assume that they really know each other simply because their "labels" imply a close relationship. Certainly a mother knows her daughter and a daughter, her mother. This is not necessarily so. The same thing could be said of other relational connections. If I call you my brother or my sister I am implying that I already know you. I assume that because we are related there is no need for us to spend time together getting to know each other.

 *Marriage is a lifelong journey into intimacy, but also into friendship.*

Labels that imply closeness and intimate knowledge may in reality hinder true relationship building. A husband and wife may assume that they know each other simply because they are married. As a result, they may do nothing more than scratch the surface, never plumbing the depths of each other's personalities to gain true knowledge and build a deep and intimate relationship.

Marriage is a lifelong journey into intimacy, but also into friendship. A husband and wife should be each other's best friend. There is no higher relationship. After all, who knows us better than our friends? Most of us will share with our friends things about ourselves that we never even tell our own families. Husbands and wives should have no secrets from each other. As their relationship develops they should grow into true friends, who know everything there is to know about each other, good and bad, and yet who love and accept each other anyway.

## No Longer Servants, but Friends

From the biblical standpoint, the highest relationship of all is that of "friend." No greater testimony could be given to the life of a biblical personality than to say that he or she was a "friend of God." Abraham fit that description: " 'Abraham believed God, and it was credited to him as righteousness,' and he was called God's friend" (Jas. 2:23b). Moses was another who knew God as a friend: "The Lord would speak to Moses face to face, as a man speaks with his friend" (Ex. 33:11a). David, the second king of Israel, was known as a man after God's own heart (see 1 Sam. 13:14). This is another way of saying that David was God's friend.

*In the Bible, the highest relationship of all is that of "friend."*

Jesus made clear in His teaching the exalted place of friendship. In the 15th chapter of the Gospel of John, after telling His followers that their intimacy with Him was like that of branches to the vine, Jesus linked that intimacy to friendship.

> *My command is this: Love each other as I have loved you. Greater love has no one than this, that he lay down his life for his friends. You are My friends if you do what I command. I no longer call you servants, because a servant does not know his master's business. Instead, I have called you friends, for everything that I learned from My Father I have made known to you* (John 15:12-15).

In these verses Jesus announces that His relationship to His followers is entering a new dimension, rising to a higher level. A fundamental change is occurring in the way they will now relate to one another. Beginning with the command to "Love each other," Jesus then describes that love, declaring that the greatest love of all is where a person is willing to "lay down his life for his friends." Jesus would demonstrate that kind of love the very next day when He went to the cross. It is significant that Jesus said "friends" here and not "family." There is a quality to true friendship that transcends and rises above even the ties of family relationships. In the Old Testament, David, the future king of Israel, and Jonathan, son of Saul, the current king, enjoyed a friendship that was deeper than family. Even as Saul sought David's life, Jonathan protected David because he was "one in spirit with David, and he loved him as himself" (1 Sam. 18:1b).

Jesus next states the new and deeper nature of the relationship: "You are My friends if you do what I command." Obedience is the test of friendship with Jesus; it is also the test of love. Jesus is not looking for obedience based on obligation such as a servant would render, but obedience based on love which grows out of the context of friendship. The first kind of obedience is imposed from without while the second kind is freely chosen from within. There is a world of difference between the two.

 *Obedience is the test of friendship with Jesus; it is also the test of love.*

In the rest of the passage Jesus draws a clear and sharp contrast between the old and new ways He and His followers will relate to each other. "I no longer call you servants, because a servant does not know his master's business. Instead, I have called you friends, for everything that I learned from my Father I have made known to you." Servants had no freedom of choice. They could not exercise their own will but were bound to do the will of their master. Rarely if ever were they privy to knowledge of the deep and intimate aspects of the life of their master or his family. Although they might live, work, eat, and sleep in their master's house, they knew nothing of his business. It was different with family and friends. They were privileged to walk in his inner circle and share in the most personal dimensions of his life.

Jesus said, "I no longer call you servants...Instead, I have called you friends..." He was telling His followers, "I do not want the kind of relationship where you are committed to Me by obligation. No more slave mentality. You are My friends, and I share everything with My friends—everything I have learned from My Father."

What was Jesus alluding to when He said, "Everything that I learned from My Father I have made known to you"? What did Jesus tell His disciples—His closest friends and followers—that He did not reveal to anyone else? He opened His heart and soul to them. He held nothing back. Jesus spoke to the multitudes in parables but later, in private with His friends, He explained everything clearly and in greater detail (see Mk. 4:33-34). He lived and worked intimately with them for three years, training and preparing them to carry on after He was no longer with them.

 *Friends share everything with each other, good or bad, happy or sad.*

One important characteristic of friends is that they share everything with each other, good or bad, happy or sad. This quality is what sets friends apart from mere acquaintances and, often, even from family members. From their earliest days together, Jesus shared with His friends all the bad or unpleasant things that would come because of their friendship. He told them that He would be betrayed, arrested, beaten, scourged, and have His beard plucked out. He would be crucified, would die and be buried, and on the third day would rise from the dead. Jesus informed His disciples that because of their friendship with Him they would be hated, despised, persecuted, and even killed. He also assured them that He would be present with them always and that they would live and walk in His power and authority. Jesus hid nothing from them. He pulled no punches and did not hedge His words. This kind of openness and transparency is the mark of true friendship.

## *Friends Are Open and Honest With Each Other*

Jesus wanted His friends to know all of this in advance so that when these things took place they would be prepared. "All this I have told you so that you will not go astray....I have told you this, so that when the time comes you will remember that I warned you" (Jn. 16:1,4a). He did not want them to be taken by surprise.

This illustrates an important truth: Friends are open and honest with each other. Nowhere is this principle more important than in a marriage relationship. One of the big problems in many marriages is that the husband and wife have trouble relating to each other as friends. They are more like "servants" than friends, more like brother and sister than husband and wife. Opening up to each other is just as difficult as opening up to family or to casual acquaintances. Most people do not share their inmost selves with their parents or siblings. They do not speak candidly about their highest dreams or their deepest fears, their greatest virtues or their worst flaws. They will, however, reveal these things to their friends. Friendship between a husband and wife, with its characteristic honesty and openness, is absolutely essential for a happy, successful, and thriving marriage.

Most couples enter married life without having told each other everything about themselves. In some ways this is to be expected. It is impossible at the beginning to be completely open and candid because some things will come out only as the relationship grows over time. Nevertheless, a couple should know as much as possible about each other—good and bad—before they stand together at the marriage altar.

The period of courtship and engagement is very valuable for this purpose. Too often, however, the man and woman will focus all their attention on always being on their best behavior for the other, careful to reveal only their good side. Out of fear of jeopardizing the budding relationship they will tiptoe around problems and avoid any mention of annoying habits or idiosyncrasies they may observe in each other. Unless they learn to be honest with each other at this stage of their relationship, they are in for a rude awakening later when, after they get married, these things inevitably come to light.

 *A couple should know as much as possible about each other—good and bad—before they stand together at the marriage altar.*

For example, if John has a problem with his temper, he should be honest with Sarah about it, and sooner rather than later. "I really struggle with my temper. I fly off the handle easily. The Lord is working with me about it, but I still have a long way to go. I just wanted to tell you so that whenever my temper flares up you will forgive me and not take it personally." This way, Sarah will not be caught completely off guard the first time John spouts off.

Sarah may struggle with feelings of jealousy or tend to be hypercritical of other people. If she is up-front and aboveboard with John about this they can waylay any misunderstanding before it starts. Together they can work on their problems and help each other grow through them and beyond them.

Obviously, any couple must feel comfortable together if this kind of honesty is to develop. Creating such a relaxed atmosphere depends a great deal on mutual respect and trust. While both of these qualities grow out of love, they also feed and nourish it. In the Bible, friendship and love are closely linked. "A friend loves at all times, and a brother is born for adversity" (Prov. 17:17). "A man of many companions may come to ruin, but there is a friend who sticks closer than a brother" (Prov. 18:24). "His mouth is sweetness itself; he is altogether lovely. This is my lover, this my friend, O daughters of Jerusalem" (Song 5:16).

Marriage is the highest of all human relationships and friendship is the highest level of that relationship. Every married couple should set their sights on rising to that level and never rest until they attain it. Even then they should not stop growing. True friendship has a breadth and a depth that no amount of time or growth can ever exhaust.

*Marriage is the highest of all human relationships and friendship is the highest level of that relationship.*

Friendship is the catalyst that ultimately will fuse a husband and wife into one like a precious gem. Marriage is an earthly, fleshly picture of the relationship in the spiritual realm between not only God the Father, God the Son—who is Jesus Christ—and God the Holy Spirit, but also between God and the race of mankind whom He created. Friendship characterizes the perfect unity and intimacy that exists among Father, Son, and Holy Spirit, and was also the nature of the relationship that Adam and Eve enjoyed with God and with each other in the Garden of Eden.

God's desire is to restore the friendship relationship between Himself and humanity that sin destroyed. The modern world desperately needs to see a clear and honest picture of what friendship with God is like. No earthly relationship comes as close to that picture as marriage, and a marriage where the husband and wife are truly friends comes closest of all.

Despite the attacks and challenges of modern society, the institution of marriage will last as long as human life on earth remains. God ordained and established marriage and it will endure until He brings all things in the physical realm to their close. No matter how much social and moral attitudes may change, marriage will remain, rock-solid as always, the best idea in human relationships ever to come down the pike, because it is God's idea.

Marriage is *still* a *great* idea!

## PRINCIPLES

1. A husband and wife should be each other's best friend. There is no higher relationship.

2. True friendship transcends and rises above even the ties of family relationships.

3. Openness and transparency are marks of true friendship.

4. Friends are open and honest with each other.

5. Friendship between a husband and wife, with its characteristic honesty and openness, is absolutely essential for a happy, successful, and thriving marriage.

5. Friendship is the catalyst that ultimately will fuse a husband and wife into one like a precious gem.

# *Exciting titles*
# by Dr. Myles Munroe

### UNDERSTANDING YOUR POTENTIAL
This is a motivating, provocative look at the awesome potential trapped within you, waiting to be realized. This book will cause you to be uncomfortable with your present state of accomplishment and dissatisfied with resting on your past success.
ISBN 1-56043-046-X

### RELEASING YOUR POTENTIAL
Here is a complete, integrated, principles-centered approach to releasing the awesome potential trapped within you. If you are frustrated by your dreams, ideas, and visions, this book will show you a step-by-step pathway to releasing your potential and igniting the wheels of purpose and productivity.
ISBN 1-56043-072-9

### MAXIMIZING YOUR POTENTIAL
Are you bored with your latest success? Maybe you're frustrated at the prospect of retirement. This book will refire your passion for living! Learn to maximize the God-given potential lying dormant inside you through the practical, integrated, and penetrating concepts shared in this book. Go for the max—die empty!
ISBN 1-56043-105-9

### SINGLE, MARRIED, SEPARATED & LIFE AFTER DIVORCE
Written by best-selling author Myles Munroe, this is one of the most important books you will ever read. It answers hard questions with compassion, biblical truth, and even a touch of humor. It, too, is rapidly becoming a best-seller.
ISBN 1-56043-094-X

### IN PURSUIT OF PURPOSE
Best-selling author Myles Munroe reveals here the key to personal fulfillment: purpose. We must pursue purpose because our fulfillment in life depends upon our becoming what we were born to be and do. *In Pursuit of Purpose* will guide you on that path to finding purpose.
ISBN 1-56043-103-2

### THE PURPOSE AND POWER OF PRAISE & WORSHIP
God's greatest desire and man's greatest need is for a Spirit-to-spirit relationship. God created an environment of His Presence in which man is to dwell and experience the fullness of this relationship. In this book, Dr. Munroe will help you discover this experience in your daily life. You are about to discover the awesome purpose and power of praise and worship.
ISBN 0-7684-2047-4

### THE PURPOSE AND POWER OF GOD'S GLORY
Everywhere we turn, we are surrounded by glory. There is glory in every tree and flower. There is the splendor in the rising and setting sun. Every living creature reflects its own glory. Man in his own way through his actions and character expresses an essence of glory. But the glory that we see in Creation is but the barest reflection of the greater glory of the Creator. Dr. Munroe surgically removes the religious rhetoric from this often-used word, replacing it with words that will draw you into the powerful presence of the Lord. *The Purpose and Power of God's Glory* not only introduces you to the power of the glory, but practically demonstrates how God longs to see His glory reflected through man.
ISBN 0-7684-2119-5

## Available at your local Christian bookstore.